Perfect Solutions for Difficult Employee Situations

Sid Kemp

D1360040

McGraw-Hill

New York Chicago San Francisco Lisbon
London Madrid Mexico City Milan New Delhi
San Juan Seoul Singapore Sydney Toronto

The McGraw·Hill Companies

Copyright © 2005 by The McGraw-Hill Companies, Inc. Printed in the United States of America. Except as permitted under the United States Copyright Act of 1976, no part of this publication may be reproduced or distributed in any form or by any means, or stored in a data base or retrieval system, without the prior written permission of the publisher.

1 2 3 4 5 6 7 8 9 0   FGR/FGR   0 9 8 7 6 5 4

ISBN 0-07-144452-1

This is a *CWL Publishing Enterprises Book* produced for McGraw-Hill by CWL Publishing Enterprises, Inc., Madison, WI, www.cwlpub.com.

 This book is printed on recycled, acid-free paper containing a minimum of 50% recycled, de-inked fiber.

This publication is designed to provide accurate and authoritative information in regard to the subject matter covered. It is sold with the understanding that neither the author nor the publisher is engaged in rendering legal, accounting, or other professional services. If legal advice or other expert assistance is required, the services of a competent professional person should be sought.
> —*From a Declaration of Principles jointly adopted by a Committee of the American Bar Association and a Committee of Publishers*

McGraw-Hill books are available at special quantity discounts to use as premiums and sales promotions, or for use in corporate training programs. For more information, please write to the Director of Special Sales, Professional Publishing, McGraw-Hill, Two Penn Plaza, New York, NY 10121-2298. Or contact your local bookstore.

Contents

Contents

Part Two. Messy Situations   23

Chapter 4. Money Issues   25

Chapter 5. When Sex Shows Up at Work   36

Contents

Contents

Contents

Contents

Contents

This one is for my dad, Bernie Kemp, who gave me a lot of support in the early years of my career, when I worked for managers who really needed to read this book.

As managers and supervisors, we cannot rely only on our own efforts to get things done. Rather, we must maximize our influence over the performance of others to be effective and achieve team goals. Because of this different dynamic—of having to get work done through others—it's vital that we continually sharpen our managerial and interpersonal skills so that the company gets the most from our team.

There are two crucial truths to consider regarding managerial effectiveness:

The leader casts a long shadow—and that shadow influences the effectiveness of the group. The leader or manager creates the tone or environment of a group. Your attitude and approach to people are contagious—they cascade throughout your team. All humans possess an open-loop emotional system in our brain that allows us to perceive and be affected by others' emotional states or moods. This is the mechanism that allows a mother to soothe her crying baby or for a giggle to infect a roomful of people. As manager, all employees' eyes are on you as you show up for the day. They are wondering, either silently or aloud,

"Is he in a good mood today? What does that frown on her face mean? Watch out—he's got that look that means we're going to have heck to pay around here today."

Your mood and emotions set the pace for the whole group. You, therefore, must be very mindful of your emotions and manage them well, because they quickly affect the entire team.

Recently, psychologists have shown that a 1% improvement in emotional climate creates a 2% increase in revenues. Yes, as the manager, you set the emotional climate of the entire group, which influences the effectiveness of your group and ultimately the profitability of your company.

Employees join companies but leave managers. I am continually struck by the number of stories that confirm the maxim that employees join companies but leave managers. Whether it's the manager who did not control her anger toward an employee or one who humiliated a team member in public, the immediate result of such a negative episode is a backwash of animosity and bad feelings toward the manager. Productivity of both the individual and the group is compromised and the ultimate result is usually a lost employee. The humiliated employee successfully seeks another position due to the lingering bad feelings about that incident or because of a pattern of similar incidents that have poisoned the relationship. And other employees seeing a manager behave this way are also more likely to leave. The result is high employee turnover, or churn.

Even in a sluggish economy in which it is relatively easy to hire new employees, the cost of losing a good employee is very high. No company can afford to lose good talent unnecessarily.

Sharpening your managerial and interpersonal skills benefits you, the manager, in the form of enhanced performance of your team and your company. The results are higher productivity and lower attrition of good talent. The examples and wisdom in *Perfect Solutions for Difficult Employee Situations* will help you become a better manager, make better contributions to the organization, and advance your career.

—Kristin Robertson

Kristin Robertson is a consultant, trainer, and author who specializes in customer service. She has helped companies such as 7-Eleven, Medtronic, Southwest Airlines, Blockbuster, and Washington Mutual. She is a frequent speaker at industry conferences and writes articles for online newsletters and trade magazines.

Preface

How to Use This Book

For fun, you can jump straight to the heart of *Perfect Solutions* and look at the messy situations in Part Two. But, before you try these solutions out on your team, be sure to read Part One: Being There. The first three chapters introduce the basic attitude and perspective that make these solutions work. I made sure that each chapter is short and to the point.

Part Two of *Perfect Solutions for Difficult Employee Situations* is full of problematic situations and the solutions for them. Each solution fits on one page and is laid out in a clear, easy-to-read format that looks like this:

An opening paragraph, describing the problematic situation and its variations.

The Situation, As a Heading

The script, one sentence to say, in italic. The script opens a paragraph in regular text with clarifications and cautions. The paragraph may contain some alternate sentences in italic. *These are alternate scripts the reader might use.* Sometimes, there are additional guidelines or processes to work through with the team member having the difficulty. Samples of dialogs that might come up appear with quotation marks.

Part Three, Too Hot to Handle discusses situations—and managerial mistakes—that can raise problems that require the help of human resources expertise, legal advice, or a shrink. Be sure to take a look—there are some situations that you would think a manager could handle, but if you talk about it the wrong way, your company could get into trouble. For example, did you know that body odor can be a medical issue and that, if you're not careful, talking with a team member about it could open you up to a lawsuit?

Special Features in This Book

Perfect Solutions for Difficult Employee Situations also includes sidebars with real-world stories that illustrate how effective these solutions have proven to be.

A note on terminology: The solutions in this book apply to any work environment—office or factory, Fortune 500 or small business, government, educational, not-for-profit, or private sector. As a result, there is no one standard term for an employee. Your company may call them *employees*, *team members*, or *direct reports*. In *Perfect Solutions for Difficult Employee Situations,* we use the terms *team member* and *employee* interchangeably.

Because I manage my own company, I encounter these situations every day. So, when making recommendations, I often say "we, as managers," meaning you and me. I hope that you will take the same collaborative, coaching approach with your team as I take with mine and with you.

Lastly, it is an unfortunate fact of the English language that there is no singular pronoun meaning "him or her." Although "he" and "him" are used extensively throughout this book, please let me assure you that all of this applies equally and identically to women—as managers and as team members—as it does to men.

Acknowledgments

Many thanks to all the members of the QTI team, past and present, who have worked with me as I've learned to be a manager and a coach for managers—my thanks for all you've taught me. And special thanks to Paul Romaine, who helped with the research for this book and who is a model of an excellent manager; to Jim Rooney, President of PeopleSmartTools and facilitator of The READ Group of Brownwood, Texas, people who were gracious enough to host me for a valuable lunch meeting and share their insights, which improved this book; and to Kristin E. Robertson of KR Consulting, for her steady, heartfelt support and her excellent foreword.

About the Author

Sid Kemp is a manager, an author, and an executive coach who specializes in applying quality processes and emotional intelligence to business situations. He has been in every embarrassing situation you can imagine—and a few you don't want to think about. (Don't ask which ones happened to him and which ones happened to his clients; he won't tell.) But if you want to be direct, friendly, and humorous about those moments we all wish just didn't happen, you won't find a better companion.

Sid is a certified Project Management Professional (PMP) and Director of Professional Development for the Alamo Chapter of the Project Management Institute. (To learn more about project management certification, go to *www.PMI.org*.) He is also a member—and former chapter board member—of the National Speakers Association (*www.NSAspeaker.org*) and a member of the Society for Human Resource Management (*www.SHRM.org*).

You can learn more about Sid and his work in corporate consulting and training and in executive coaching with emotional intelligence at *www.qualitytechnology.com*.

Part One

Being There

Part One of *Perfect Solutions for Difficult Employee Situations* provides you with the perspective of perfect solutions—respect the person and solve the business problem. The fundamental approach of this book is cooperative and collaborative. Respecting each team member means putting that person into the driver's seat—and teaching him or her to steer. Our team succeeds when each person does his share. Our job is to help and encourage each person to see the goal and pull in the right direction. And, unfortunately, to be realistic when an individual can't or won't work with the team and help us reach that goal.

Managers are people, too. If we don't take good care of ourselves and respect ourselves, we will burn out, just like anyone else. When we are fried, we can't serve up the perfect solution. So, Chapter 1, Facing Your Day, is for you—it gives you the tools of self-renewal and focus that let you be there for your team.

Chapter 2, From Challenges to Solutions, teaches the basic art of reframing—how to shift perspective and help others do the same—which is a key technique for many of the solutions. Sometimes, a problem looks big only because we are kneeling in front of it. When we stand up and face the problem, it becomes smaller and more manageable.

Part One ends with Chapter 3, The Manager's Survival Guide, which lays out the way to a perfect solution. Classically, tragedies end up with everyone dying and comedies end up with the problem solved and everyone happy. If we see each difficult situation as the beginning of a real-life drama, then our job is to direct and act in that drama to make it into a comedy—a set of actions that solve the problem and keep the team together. To get from problem to solution, we need to work through a series of steps with our team, just as a comedy must move through several scenes to a happy ending.

Chapter 1
Facing Your Day

This chapter takes a look at the things any manager can do to be ready for the embarrassing and difficult employee problems that show up unexpectedly and pile up because we don't want to look at them.

Remember: You Matter

Our basic approach to management is "Care for the person, take care of the problem." And the first person you need to care for is you. I'm not encouraging self-centeredness; I'm encouraging effectiveness. If you feel good—if your energy is up, your mind is clear, and you have a positive focus—then you will be a better manager. And you will be more able to handle difficult situations.

Psychologically, emotional intelligence studies show that an optimistic realism is the healthiest and most effective outlook on life. Anyone in business can understand the value of realism—it pays to see things as they are and deal with them. What is the justification for optimism? Simply this: people can solve problems. People can face difficult situations and make them better. That's the basis for adding a bit of optimism to our realism.

Physically, we are more attentive, and therefore more effective, when we are relaxed, well rested, and free of pain. If we are tapped out, stretching ourselves with caffeine, or not getting enough exercise, we are simply less ready for work. A manager's difficult situation is a sprinter's 100-yard dash. Are you ready to run?

Take good care of yourself. And, if you haven't developed habits for doing that every day, start now. Speaking from experience, it's a lot harder to develop those habits later, after you burn out and have to restart your life and your career.

Focus First

I called Part One of this book *Being There* because full, focused attention is the first key to success. The runner thinks only about the race. The artist considers only the scene he is painting. The engineer or architect must focus on her work without interruption. It is time to realize that the same is true for managers and leaders. When we have a clear, single focus, we deal with difficult situations well. And that takes practice.

The best practice is to begin each day with time spent breathing, relaxing, and focusing. If you can't take time out, you can do it while you drive or while you walk from your car to your office.

The simplest exercise is *stop, breathe, restart.* To stop means to bring the mind to this moment, to stop worrying about the future or the past or anyone who isn't with us right here, right now. No thoughts. Without thoughts, we breathe and we feel our breath. Do this right now. As you're reading this book, stop and breathe three times, feeling your breath. Then turn your attention to the next sentence.

If you do this while driving, turn off the radio or the tape player. Watch the road. Feel your body in the seat, your hands on the wheel, your feet on the pedals. Watch where you are going. You're not only being a safer driver; you're also preparing yourself for the day. If you do it while walking, notice the sky or the clouds or a lovely tree.

What you focus on isn't important. What matters is that you are learning to focus on the situation you are in, to focus on whatever is right in front of you. It sounds silly, but it takes practice. Once you practice it for a few days, you'll see how effective it is.

Or, you can prove it right now, in your own experience.

1. Remember a time when you wanted to talk to someone about something important, but they were distracted and didn't really listen. How did you feel?
2. Remember another time when you wanted to talk about something important and someone gave you their full attention and took you seriously. How did you feel?
3. As a manager, you have dozens of opportunities each day to be like the first person or like the second.
4. The lesson: If you want people to be influenced by you, be there for them, be attentive and present, and take their perspective seriously. Then they are much more likely to respond well to what you have to say.

The Manager Who Wasn't There

When I was in my early 20s, I had a boss who had weekly meetings with each of his managers, one on one, on Thursday mornings. I met with the boss right after he met with a guy he didn't like. The boss appeared to be listening, but he was always distracted and irritated. At first, I thought he didn't like me, but the problem didn't show up any other time. Then I realized that he wasn't really listening to me. The boss was running one hour behind—reacting emotionally to the guy before me, while sitting there with me.

I saw then and there I wasn't going to get anywhere with this guy. If he couldn't be present and listen, how could he hear what I had to say or give any real attention to my problems or my successes? I moved on and left that job not too long after.

The lesson: If you want to keep good team members and help low performers improve, be present for each one, each moment of the day.

Each Person Is a Treasure ... with Problems

Sometimes, it seems like a person is the problem. Think about the guy before me in the story of the weekly meetings, above. I'm sure the boss thought, before every meeting with that guy, *Oh, no, not him again. He challenges my authority every time we meet.* And, most of the time, he was right. What is more difficult to see is the manager's mistake—we see what we focus on.

There are sayings that remind us of this: *A hammer sees everything as a nail* and, my favorite, *A pickpocket among saints sees only their pockets.*

Learn a lesson from gardening. Weeds and flowers both grow, but if we nourish the flowers and pull the weeds, we get a beautiful garden. Nourish the flowers—the skills and good qualities of your team members—with your attention. Point out the weeds and let the team members pull them up themselves. That's how we cultivate a highly productive team.

We all have qualities that are good for work and others that get in the way of work. We all have flowers and weeds. *Each person is a treasure, with problems.* By focusing on the treasure, we remember the reason we put up with the problems while the team member works them through.

Be a Practical Idealist

Hardly a month goes by without someone reminding me that I'm an idealist. And they're right. Ultimately, I believe in each person's ability to overcome his or her difficulties and show forth wonderful gifts.

But, in a business context, the key word is sometimes "ultimately." When a really difficult situation comes up, I face the question: Even if this person can ultimately do a good job, can he do it on time for *this* job? The bottom line can't always wait for the development of human potential.

I work with people as optimistically as I can, within the real limits of the budget and time of the business.

What are the key signs that an employee is worth keeping through a difficult situation? If an employee has these four qualities, things can work out:

- Willingness to solve the problem and do a good job
- Clarity about the problem and what he has to do
- Complete honesty and a willingness to discuss anything relevant
- The ability to solve the problem within the time available

With these four elements, you have the basis of success. If those are the ingredients, then the perfect solutions in this book are the recipe. And we cook by:

1. Bringing up the issue
2. Listening to the team member and making a connection
3. Defining the difficult situation
4. Designing an action plan, with clear steps to take, results to deliver, and due dates
5. Following through to make sure the team member adheres to the plan and delivers the results

That's the whole process, in a nutshell. You can think of the solutions in Part Two as a way to deal with all kinds of nuts.

Come Up for Air, and Dive in Again

So, I've taught you to start your day fresh. How long will that last? On a typical day—about 10 minutes. But being a manager is a lot like being a basketball player. Each play matters when it is happening, but when it's over, it's gone, whether you scored or not. Move on to the next play. Get the ball. Make the shot. Start over.

Let's take a look at that last. How do we start over? Watch a basketball player shake his head and catch his breath after each play. Make that: Stop, take a few breaths, get clear, start over.

Many of my coaching clients are therapists. When a therapist becomes a client, the first thing I teach him or her is what to do in the 10 minutes between sessions. You guessed it: Stop, breathe, take care of yourself, restart. The greatest gift a therapist can give his clients is genuine attention and presence. With that, people often heal themselves. Without it, even prescriptions are often of no value, because it's too easy to give the wrong prescription.

Facing Your Day

Always give yourself at least three breaths—and a few minutes if you can—between one person—one problem—and the next. Clear your mind—shake out your body, if you have to—stop, breathe, and restart.

It's like swimming underwater. There are pearls to gather, but you have to come up for air, and dive in again. With practice, you'll find that you stay fresh and energetic all day long.

Chapter 2
From Challenges to Solutions
Looking at Life from Both Sides

S ometimes, it's your perspective that makes the situation difficult. When you watch a movie, you never see the camera, but it is always there. It is on the stage and the actors are aware of it, paying attention to it, working with it. The camera is focused on the action, but the actors are focused on the camera.

In the same way, when you look at a situation, you're focusing on the problem, but your team may be focusing on you. You are part of the picture, and if you don't see and understand the effect of your own perspective, your own perspective can make a situation difficult. If you know where you stand, you can get out of the way or you can move a little bit, see past the obstruction, and see the solution.

This chapter teaches reframing, a basic, quick technique for handling old problems in a new way. Business speak offers many other terms similar to reframing, including "shifting paradigms" and "thinking outside the box." Whatever we call it, it's easy to do—and it works.

Seeing Yourself

Before we can think outside the box, we have to know what box we're in. For me, the first sign of a difficult situation is often that I feel frustrated. Others might feel confused or might put the situation completely out of their minds. If you see any of these happening, it's a good idea to get clear by writing down the answers to these questions:

- What is the situation? Do I even know enough to say what the situation is?
- Who's involved?
- Am I thinking that a team member is the problem, so that I'm not on the same side with him?
- Am I thinking that I'm the problem, that I should be able to take care of this, but I'm not up to the job?
- What makes this situation difficult to handle? Is it complicated? Can I just see no solution? Or do I see a solution, but I don't believe the team member can get there?

Find out where you are and what the situation is. This will be the starting point for the perfect solution. For example, each of these situations might look the same at first, but should be approached differently:

- An employee is frequently late because he has a child with health problems.
- An employee is frequently late. You think it is a family problem, but you're not sure.
- An employee is frequently late, and you just don't know why.

As you will see in Part Two, each of these situations has a different solution—because the perfect solution starts where we are, not where you wish you were. One big challenge for many managers is admitting, *I don't know enough about what is going on.* We feel we should know, that it's part of our job. I look at it a little differently: *Knowing what's going on is part of my job. So, if I don't know, I'll ask.* This is very appropriate for situations involving the personal lives, attitudes, stress, and perspectives of our team members. These are things we can't know about—and perhaps shouldn't know about—except when they get mixed up with work. Starting where we are sometimes means being willing to acknowledge what we don't know and being willing to open up and learn more about a situation.

Changing Your Stance

Once we know our own stance, we can decide if we need to change it. Are we ready to work with the team member and face the problem? If not—if we're still blaming someone or taking the position of a victim—then we need to change our stance before we meet with the team member.

Chapter 3, The Manager's Survival Guide, will give you a process and several techniques for changing your stance. They all have one crucial quality: the shift has to be genuine. If I suggest you change the words you use, you can't change just the words. It is essential to change your perspective—your thoughts, feelings, and point of view—as well as your words.

You can think outside the box only if you know what box you are in. A director can tell the cameraman to move only if he steps back and sees that the camera is in the way. That is why it is so important to use the bulleted list of questions above and to write down your answers. Once you step back and see your perspective, it is easy to change it. If you see you're blaming the team member, then stop. Stop, breathe, step outside the box, and restart.

Changing the Situation

Once you aren't part of the problem, you become part of the solution. But only part of it. The team member with the difficult situation will always be the central player—the star actor. Your job, then, is to be director, script writer, coach. Help the team member see a different way of seeing things and a different way of acting that will resolve the situation. That takes less effort than doing it yourself. More importantly, it builds the team, because you are helping people do good work and solve their problems, rather than acting like a parent and taking their work away from them every time they have a problem.

Just like you, your team members need to see where they are before they can change their approach. You can help by asking questions, understanding the situation, and helping them to see it in a new light. Then you can build a plan to a solution and stay with them while they follow the plan. A team effort with a clear plan is the solution to most difficult situations. A few of them are even easier—you just need a change of perspective, a good laugh, and a fresh start.

Chapter 3
The Manager's Survival Guide

Actually, this chapter is much more than a survival guide. It gives you the core technique for developing an effective coaching style of management and for moving from being a manager to being a leader. What's the difference? Managers manage people's work. Leaders teach people to be self-managed and to work together toward common goals. Leadership is a quality that keeps team members loyal to the manager so that they stay with the company—meeting goals, reducing costs, and improving the bottom line. Learn the steps in this chapter and you will have a greater chance of being a star, instead of being head of a department constantly seen as a "problem child," where high costs and churn create an endless losing battle.

This chapter teaches the approach that makes every one of these scripts work. I'm going to ask you to pay close attention and practice the steps. Why? Because *even a perfect solution has to be delivered well. And the key to good delivery is being genuine. Be there for the team member, person to person. At the same time, work on the problem, and solve it.*

Imagine that you went to the best restaurant in town and ordered the perfect meal—the one that was just right for you that day. You see the waiter coming with the tray and you're full of pleasant anticipation. And then he drops the plate in your lap! The perfect meal—delivered badly. That is what it will be like for your team if you deliver the solutions from this book without taking the time to focus, to care about your team member, to connect with him as he faces this problem with you.

Instead, follow the seven steps in this chapter and deliver the perfect solution.

1. Start by not understanding.
2. Relax and be with the person, not the problem.
3. Listen and dig deeper.
4. Create a no-blame environment.
5. Use the sandwich.
6. Decorate the sandwich.
7. Add the dessert.

Take these steps to solve the problem and strengthen the team.

Start by Not Understanding

Sometimes, we think we know exactly what the situation is. I'm going to suggest two things:

- If we have the slightest hesitation about our understanding, we should ask. Anything the team member tells us will clarify the situation and make sure we start off without putting our foot in our mouth.
- Even if we understand the situation perfectly, that isn't as important as having the team member understand it. And

people understand something said in their own words better than the same thing said the way you would say it. Also, we express respect by listening first, before we speak. Even when you understand a situation, I recommend asking the employee to explain his view first. If his view is correct, you can affirm it. If it is off, you can say you understand, then provide some course correction. Either way, by taking a position of not knowing, by listening first, you build a stronger relationship and increase the chances that the team member will listen to you, make the right decision, and follow through.

For this reason, you will see that many of the solutions begin with phrases like *Tell me what happened* or *I want to talk about* .... In opening the door this way, we allow the team member to be heard—and feel understood—first. This helps the team member relax and be more open to our perspective and our solution.

Relax and Be with the Person, Not the Problem

Suppose you were an athletic coach, training a cross-country runner. One day, you might run alongside him, talking about his running style and his strategy. You'd relax and run right at his side, being there with him. That would allow you to talk, to connect—and to keep moving toward a solution. If you stayed back at the starting gate, you wouldn't be able to talk to him.

Remember: the difficult situation—the problem—is where you want to start. And you want to go with the team member, leave the problem behind, and focus on the solution. If you stay focused on the problem, you never leave the starting gate. So, focus on being with the team member. Develop the solution with the team member and keep him pointed in the right direction.

Listen and Dig Deeper

Remember: the most important part of the solution is the team member's understanding of and commitment to the work that will get him to the goal. *Your understanding and commitment aren't all that important, unless you can share them with your team. They have to carry the load and cross the goal line.* You can increase understanding and commitment in others through:

- Your clarity in understanding the solution
- Your sympathy for feelings of embarrassment, fear, inadequacy, or anger
- Offering simple steps to take
- Sharing your vision of the solution
- Offering your presence and encouragement

Many of these gifts can be delivered through silence—the silence of listening. Allow the team member to develop his or her own understanding. Then affirm, correct, and guide it. People are most committed to their own plans.

In business, all plans should be in writing. So, after listening, write a plan—a short series of steps, with delivery dates for each one—with the team member. This reduces future conflict as you guide and encourage the team member all the way to a successful solution.

Create a No-Blame Environment

Perfect solutions are part of a larger approach to leadership and management. A humanistic perspective on management encourages *valuing people and solving problems.* One key to this is to understand that blame is not helpful, because the people are not the problem. As a result, I encourage my clients to build a no-blame environment for their team.

Our own attitude toward our work and our team creates the *no-blame environment*. If we focus on the reality of work and results, and not on personalities and blame, we take the first step. As shown in Table 3-1, we take the second step by making sure that each person has what is needed to do the job, so that responsibility and accountability are matched with authority, empowerment, ability, skills, knowledge, and resources. When the work environment has a balance of responsibility and empowerment, then each person's job is realistic and we can focus on reality and success, not personality and blame.

When we create this balance, each person on the team takes on a job and has what is needed to do that job. If we do this, then work gets done and deadlines are met. If problems come up, we work together to resolve them. There is no need to ask who's to blame when something goes wrong.

Creating the no-blame environment is an ongoing team effort—and you have to lead the way. People make mistakes and misunderstand one another. We are part of those mistakes and misunderstandings. And we are also part of good work and success. And so is everyone else.

Taking these six steps, you will transform your company or department into a productive no-blame work environment.

1. Recognize that blame exists. We create it together, and we can work to eliminate it together.
2. Recognize that blame adds nothing to the bottom line. Blame is like static—it interferes with communication, slowing things down and cutting into productivity.
3. Commit to a team environment based on respect, and based on the idea that everyone is an adult who wants to do a good job.

Reality-Based	Personality-Based
Responsibility for actions and their consequences	Blame for failure
Accountability for results	Personal praise
	Politics (in the negative sense of the term)
Supported and Balanced by	Avoidance of responsibility
	Micromanagement
Clear job definition	Denial
Authority	Manipulation
Empowerment	Anger
Ability	Criticism
Skills and tools	Excuses
Knowledge, information, and methods	
Resources, including • People • Money • Information systems • Information, including status and technical specifications	

Table 3-1. Views of the work environment: reality vs. personality

4. Work structurally, using Table 3-1, views of the work environment, to create and maintain a no-blame environment.
5. Set up regular, effective meetings for status reports, to set direction and to clear the air.

19

6. Receive status reports with appreciation for learning the truth, even if the news is bad news.

When we leave blame out of the picture, the team can focus on delivering the work. We can eliminate the negative aspects of dealing with personality. That allows the team to focus on the real gifts of personality, the unique qualities each team member brings to the job, improving the results.

Use the Sandwich

People tend to expect blame when a difficult situation has come up. So, even in a no-blame environment, we need to deliver bad news—or discuss difficult situations—in a special way that establishes safety. This approach is called the *sandwich*. It is very simple: we put the bad news in between two slices of good news.

We don't have to think up two slices of good news; the sandwich is much easier than that:

- The first slice of good news is *I appreciate having you as part of the team and I know we can work this out.*
- The center of the sandwich is the difficult situation.
- The second slice of good news is *We'll build a plan together and I'll help you follow through to success.*

What do you do if the team member is on probation or you're not sure he really can work it out? Then change the first slice by saying, *"I'm here to help you work this out and I believe you can do it."*

Decorate the Sandwich

What do you do if this is not the first time this difficult situation has come up with the team member? Do what fancy restaurants do—decorate the sandwich to get attention. Restaurants use parsley; you can use delivery dates. (I don't call them *deadlines*; that sounds too fatalistic.) Be very clear about what needs to be done and when it needs to be done—whether it's a change of behavior or a piece of work—and you can stay on the same side with the team member while requiring real change. You might say, *"The department [or the project] needs this to be done by [date]."*

Add the Dessert

If—I'd like to say *when*—the team member delivers, changing the habit or resolving the situation—real appreciation is due. If the situation was difficult for you, then think what it was like for the team member! Real growth and learning, as well as good work, were involved. Appreciate the good work and let the employee know what the reward is. The reward may be as small as a thank-you and a bit of relief or it may be as large as a chance to keep his job or get a promotion. Whatever it is, acknowledge the success and help the team member and the team move on to the next step.

Part Two

Messy Situations

E ach chapter in Part Two gives solutions for about 10 difficult situations. Topics range from love and sex to respect in the office to handling conflicts about money. Each tip includes the difficult situation, the script for the solution, and some extra advice. We've added sidebars and stories to clarify the key points of each chapter.

If you are facing a difficult situation, you can turn to the appropriate chapter and flip through the pages to find the situation and its solution. If you are generally interested in a topic, you can read through the chapter. In general, each chapter is organized with easier situations first and more difficult ones later.

As you read each situation, feel free to use it as is. Or, you can adapt it to the details of your team member's circumstances and personality. Making the solution your own conveys your sincere interest in helping the team member create the solution.

Chapter 4
Money Issues

W hat do you do when an employee wants a raise and deserves one and you can't give it? What do you do when an employee wants a raise and doesn't deserve it? What do you do when an employee is making more money than you are and you feel envy? When you have to announce a pay cut? Money matters, but jobs aren't all about money. We'll show you how to defuse and respond to money problems with employees.

A Team Member Deserves a Raise, but That Isn't Possible

In this situation, a team member—through good work or through staying with the company long enough—has earned a raise, but the company has a pay freeze or just doesn't have enough money to pay people more right now.

Be sure to go to bat for your team. If there isn't an official pay freeze, let the boss or HR know this person deserves a raise. Even if there is an official freeze, be sure to recognize the employee to the boss and try to get a statement such as "If we were giving raises right now, your team member would be sure to get one."

Then you are ready to speak to the team member. *You deserve a raise, but the company can't do that right now.* Listen to his response. If you can get any other information—such as when the freeze is likely to end and whether annual pay increases will be retroactive—be sure to do so. Ask the employee if there is anything you can do that is within your power that would recognize his value to the team and the company.

A Team Member Doesn't Deserve a Raise, but Thinks He or She Does

Your work is valuable, but we don't see eye to eye on a raise. Then, turn to the specifics. Listen to the team member and acknowledge what he or she has done well. If the position already has a clear, measurable, up-to-date job description, compare his performance with that and let him know what he needs to do to get a raise. Include an affirmation of current good work by saying, *"Keep doing this the way you are, you're good at it."* Add other specific items by saying, *"To deserve a raise, you need to do this, too."*

Define an evaluation period and arrange for a meeting to evaluate the employee's work at the end of that period. Make the evaluation criteria as clear and objective as possible. And make sure you have the authority to give the raise when the employee earns it.

Don't wait to the end of the period to perform the evaluations. A good manager meets with each team member weekly or monthly to keep everyone going in the right direction.

This Timesheet—or Expense Report—Doesn't Look Right

You think an employee has put false or inaccurate information on a time sheet or an expense report.

Before you do anything, evaluate the seriousness of the problem:

- Check enough timesheets or expense reports to see if this is a one-time event or an ongoing problem.
- Use your judgment to decide if you think the wrong information was the result of an error or if it was intentional.
- Decide how confident you are that the information really is incorrect.

If you suspect ongoing falsification of records, that's fraud. Talk to HR or legal counsel before you speak to the employee.

If you think that it is an error or a minor one-time effort at padding, approach it as if it is an error. *This timesheet—or expense report—doesn't look right.* Ask him or her to explain it to you step by step. If the employee corrects the error or straightens out the problem, say, *"Thanks. Please try to be more careful next time."* That way, if it was an error, he knows to be more careful. If it was a trick, he knows you are watching.

Other problems may turn up. It may be that the expense report was accurate, but some rule or limit was exceeded. In that case, work with the employee or an assistant to write up clear instructions and guidelines for timesheets and expense reports and make sure everyone gets a copy.

An Employee Asks for an Advance

As a general rule, advances are a bad idea. Here's why:

- They mix the core of a business—money—with the team member's personal life and personal financial situation.
- No matter how confident you are that the employee is telling the truth, it may not be the whole truth.
- If something unexpected happens and the employee can't pay back, then it leads to a great deal of trouble.

So, give an advance only if:

- The employee has already done the work that earns the advance.
- It is very clearly a one-time situation.
- The amount is small and can be made up in the next paycheck.

EXAMPLE: A LEGITIMATE ADVANCE

Let's say that an employee gets paid every two weeks, with the check arriving a week after the end of the pay period. On the Monday of the second week of the pay period, the employee comes to you and says that his wallet, with a lot of cash and all his credit cards, was stolen over the weekend. He shows you the police report he filed.

In this case, it would make sense to give the employee one week's pay that day, as an advance on his next paycheck.

Announcing Pay Cuts and Pay Freezes

The company has decided it can't afford planned increases in compensation or even needs to cut people's pay. Unfortunately, it's your job to tell the team.

If everyone is affected more or less equally, bring everyone together at once. If only some people are affected, speak to each one individually, but meet with them back to back so that rumors don't have time to spread.

There are three things you can do to prepare:

- *Assess your own situation first.* Are you affected by the cut? If not, can you show something you are doing—maybe working extra hours without compensation—that is helping the company through the crisis?
- *Get the facts together.* The better everyone understands the situation, the less likely there will be complaints that the company is doing fine and just greedy. Also, people will want to know what their new paychecks will be and how long the situation will last.
- *Evaluate the situation.* Did you have a part in the decision? Do you agree with it? Is there a history of conflict between management and employees that could explode?

The company is having a hard time, and we all need to give something. Then explain the facts and consequences. Then listen. Through compassionate, active listening, help employees think through the consequences in their own lives. Be on their side, but don't take sides against the company. If a team member is being hostile to the company, encourage a more positive approach: *It's better to get ahead than to get even.*

However, if you are not satisfied that the company is being fair, then it is probably better to be honest about that. *I don't fully agree with this decision, but, in this department, we're a team and we'll pull together.*

EXAMPLE: PAY CUTS BROUGHT THE TEAM TOGETHER

One of my clients is managing his company through a very hard time that has gone on for several years. After a corporate partner left, he tried to pull the team together, but the memories of difficulty and conflict left everyone hesitant. Changes in the industry reduced income drastically and the owner had to make pay cuts to keep the company afloat. He had tried for several months to let his team know how bad things were, but they hadn't really wanted to listen.

He realized that he needed to cut one person to part time and give everyone else a 20% pay cut. He called me up and we brainstormed how to tell the team. I suggested that he present all the facts he faced and then his choice: he could either close up shop or make these drastic cost reductions. And then he said that he wanted to keep going and wanted to keep the team with him.

He did. Seeing their own pay affected, the team finally got the message. They accepted the cuts and actually refocused and got more productive, working to save the company.

Announcing Layoffs

Sometimes, we have to let people go. A project may be finished or a company may be shrinking. Perhaps we made the decision or participated in it. It's particularly difficult if we chose who was to be laid off. But it's never easy.

Start with *The company needs to lay you off.* Then add a reason that makes it clear it is not personal. Examples include:

- A certain number of people had to go and you had the least time with the company.
- The project you've been working on was cancelled.

Be prepared to explain the details of departure date, final pay, and unemployment benefits or direct the team member to HR for that information. If several people are being laid off, talk with each separately, but have one good-bye party for all.

It is equally important to talk to the team members who remain. If you are confident that there will be no more layoffs for a period of time, let them know that. People cannot work well if they don't know when the ax is going to fall. If you don't know what is going to happen, focus on what the team can do and promise to keep everyone informed regularly. Then do keep people informed, even if it's just to call everyone together and say there is no news. When a company is downsizing, no news is good news—as long as you tell everyone that there's no news.

EXAMPLE: A COMPASSIONATE LAYOFF

When I was just out of college and unemployment was over 10%, I worked as a temporary typist. One job required very fast data entry on a complicated accounts receivable system. I didn't have the right training and I wasn't able to do the job. At the end of the first week, the manager told me it was my last day.

I had been counting on that job to give me enough money to visit my parents. I went out back on my lunch break and cried. He came out, sat beside me, and listened to me. He let me know that there was nothing wrong with me—the other folks had been doing this kind of work for years.

Now, over 20 years later, I still remember his kindness. Are you the kind of manager employees will remember in 20 years?

Announcing a Change in Benefits

Changes in medical plans, retirements, and other parts of the benefits package are extremely complicated. Changes can include an increase in total cost, an increase in cost to the employee, and changes in who is covered, what is covered, and what medical providers are allowed. How the change affects each person depends on the size of the team member's family and many other factors.

This is not your territory. If your company has an HR department, have the team members speak directly with them. If not, hire an HR consultant or have a representative of your benefits plan hold a meeting for the team; be sure to allow time for individual questions and assistance with forms or other requirements. A good introduction might be *This is a big change and I don't understand it much better than you do. I wouldn't want to make a mistake. Why don't you talk with [name of contact]?*

"He Makes More Than I Do"

Sometimes, a team member may complain about what looks like an unfair situation around pay or benefits.

It is important to start with company policy. In some organizations, such as state agencies, pay is a matter of public record. In others, it is supposed to be confidential. And many companies lie somewhere in between.

If company policy is not to breach confidentiality and discuss these matters, say, *"It's unfortunate you found this out, and we really shouldn't discuss it."* You can go on by saying, "Because pay is confidential, I don't have enough information to discuss this with you, and I'm not allowed to, anyway. But I can discuss your compensation with you. Aside from what you heard about the other team member, do you think your pay is fair for what you do?"

If the matter is open for discussion, say, *"There are many things that go into making a person's current pay. Let's take a look and see what is happening."* Sometimes, it is a matter of longevity with the company, prior experience or education, initial salary negotiation, or some particular aspect of the job description. Show the team member the complexities of the situation, then redirect him back to his own situation—what can he do to increase his pay?

Sometimes, you may have to apply this remedy to yourself. Managers occasionally find that people on their own team—especially commissioned salespeople and technical experts—make more than we do. Remember: *Fairness isn't about comparison; it's about a win for each person. Don't ask, "What's he getting?" Instead, ask, "Am I getting what I want?"*

Chapter 5
When Sex Shows Up at Work

People are people, and if we didn't enjoy sex, then we wouldn't have lasted three million years. But sex and romance at the office can create real problems. At best, sex takes the focus away from work. At worst, sexual harassment leads to costly lawsuits. And the manager is the company's first line of defense.

Be aware of any company policy relating to personal relationships. Some companies don't allow them at all; others have no rules. In between, there is a range, from not allowing such relationships between a superior and a direct report to not allowing them within one office. Aside from the rules, your job is to respect people's personal lives while making sure that the office is for work and that their personal lives—when they go well or when they turn sour—don't get in the way of work.

It's Getting a Little Hot in Here

You think—or you know—that two people on your team are getting romantically interested or becoming an item. Maybe you're unsure or maybe it's all too clear and graphic. In either case, plan to talk to each one of them separately and not one right after the other.

It's getting a little hot in here. Then say, "It seems like" or "It's pretty clear that you and [name the other person] are developing some kind of personal relationship. I want to talk to each of you about it separately."

If there are rules that apply, then inform them of the rules. Open with a phrase like "In case you don't know," rather than telling them they should know the rules or assuming they don't.

Whether or not rules apply, focus on specific behavior and on the effect that behavior has on work. Be clear if you are concerned about their work or the work of other people in the office. Help them understand the consequences and the needs of the office. Then let them decide on a course of action to ensure that their personal lives don't get in the way of the office's work.

Here are some specific situations that might come up:

■ The couple is having personal conversations, or even arguments, that distract others from work.

■ The couple is sharing intimate details, stories of their dates, and/or passing notes, in ways that create an uncomfortable or inappropriately sexualized work environment.

■ The two people are taking breaks from work and disappearing together to deal with personal issues or have personal time together during work hours.

Help the couple understand how those behaviors are uncomfortable for others to see and how they interfere with work. Follow up by setting a deadline for the change of behavior the couple agrees to and then meeting with them—together or separately, as they prefer—to let them know if they've done enough or if more is needed.

No Bedding Down in the Office

A couple was caught "doing it" in the office. It doesn't matter whether they were same sex or different sex, whether it was during work hours or after work hours. Your challenge is to help everyone let go of a highly embarrassing situation, and humor is the key.

No bedding down in the office. Say it like a rule, but with a smile. If everyone knows what happened, talk to the couple together; otherwise, speak with them separately. Then say that, whether this was the only time it happened, it must be the last time it happens. Be clear that after-hours isn't OK and neither is the company parking lot. They need to keep their personal and sexual lives thoroughly separate from the office from now on.

If they are embarrassed and responsive, there is no need to talk about consequences. If you are not sure that they are taking the situation seriously, think through the consequences and let them know what will happen if it happens again.

In the unlikely case that you hear something like "We're not the only ones doing this," then say, "Thanks for letting me know. I'll make sure everyone knows about the new rule."

By focusing on the present and future, you make room for people to let go of their embarrassment. It may be appropriate to meet with the person or people who caught them at it, let them know that you've spoken to the couple, and to listen to their feelings, as well.

"You're Interested, but She or He Isn't"

A team member comes to you and lets you know that another team member is expressing interest in a romantic or sexual relationship and that the advances are not wanted. The first team member asks you to speak to the other one and you agree to do so.

[Name of teammate] asked me to tell you he/she isn't interested. The person you're speaking with may say that he never intended to express interest. Say, *"I'm glad. Now that you know you've been misunderstood, please apologize to her and make sure you don't give the wrong impression again."*

If the person doesn't want to believe there is no reciprocal interest, say, *"She/He couldn't make it clear enough herself. That's why she/he asked me to tell you."*

At this point, shift to implications for work. *I want each member of my team to feel comfortable, so we can all focus on work and work together.* That will probably be sufficient. But, if it isn't, the next step is *What you are doing could be interpreted as sexual harassment, and that's a big problem for all of us.*

In some cases, the team member may be compliant, but be unaware of what he or she is doing that appears to the other person to be an advance. In that case, tell the team member, *"Talk only about work and be careful not to touch him/her."*

"He or She Won't Leave Me Alone"

When you hear this from a team member, you know that the person feels pressured, perhaps even persecuted, by a coworker's attention. It may be that the other person won't take "no" for an answer or that the two used to have a relationship and there are still hurt feelings or that the person's behavior is, for cultural or other reasons, offensive to the team member who is complaining.

What's he/she doing? is a good start. Get a clear picture of the words or actions that create discomfort, how often it happens, and where it happens. *Have you told him/her to stop?* is a good next step. Sometimes people think they convey a clear "no," but really don't. Do your best to have the team member clear this up himself or herself. But, if that doesn't work, see above, "You're Interested, but He or She Isn't."

When talking with the team member who is making the complaint, try to get a sense of how serious or painful this is. Does the team member see it as sexual harassment? Do you? If the team member doesn't mention the idea, but you think of it, don't mention it to the team member. But do feel free to say something like *[The other person] is breaking the rules, and I'll let him know it and tell him to stop.*

Be cautious about three other possible situations:

- The complaints could go both ways. If the two people are fighting or bickering, both might feel harassed.
- The person might have a legitimate sexual harassment complaint. In that case, get guidance from HR or legal counsel.

- If the team member who is complaining says that several people are being difficult, be aware of the problem of *mobbing*, which is discussed in Chapter 7, Pranks, Put-Downs, and Bending the Rules.

There is one more thing that may be happening—and it can be very touchy. Sometimes people unwittingly draw unwanted attention to themselves by the way they dress, the way they speak, or their body language. However, if you mention this, you can sound like you are blaming the victim. There are two ways to handle this situation:

- **Create a rule.** If a certain type of clothing is provocative, let everyone know that you'd rather not have anyone wear it.
- **Provide cautious advice.** Do this only after you have spoken to the people who are acting inappropriately. After this, you can go back to the complainant and say something like "Their behavior was wrong, and I've told them. But there is something you can do to help. I think they may be reacting to some of the things you talk about. I realize that you have the right to talk about anything you want to, but if you could stop talking about your personal activities at work, the whole team might get along better."

"You're Interested, but I'm Not"

A team member has expressed interest in spending personal time with you, in romantic involvement or in a sexual relationship. You don't want to go there—whether for personal reasons or professional ones.

Be sure not to make assumptions. Unless it is clear that the other person is interested, say something like *I get that you might be interested in a personal relationship, aside from our work time together. Am I right?* Give the other person a chance to clarify—or to backpedal.

If you can, use an objective rule as your reason for not going further. (For a list of sources of rules, see the next section, "Uh-oh, I'm Interested.") If office romance is OK and your reasons are purely personal, still try to make it impersonal, saying something like *I don't want to mix work and pleasure, it's too risky*, or simply *This isn't a good time for me.*

Uh-oh, I'm Interested

Here, you find yourself romantically interested in someone on your team. It is time for some deep self-evaluation.

First, do no harm is what you should say to yourself. Then ask, *What are the rules?* and *What is the big picture?*

Rules come from four places:

- From the company or office
- From ethical guidelines we accept as part of our professional association membership
- From our life outside the office, including our personal life and religious values
- From within ourselves

When we ask ourselves, *"What is the big picture?"* that includes:

- What effect does this have on the office and on work?
- What effect does this have on other team members?
- What effect does this have on my own family life? On my job?

We need to consider the effect of a relationship and also the effect of the relationship not working out. For example, if you express personal interest in a team member and it is not reciprocated, problems can follow. If, later, you decide not to give that team member an opportunity, a promotion, or a raise, even for good reasons, you're open to a claim of sexual harassment.

Your challenge is this: *Respect your feelings, but don't let them control what you do.* This can lead to one of three resolutions:

- If you decide that moving toward a relationship is not the right thing to do, and you think that the other person doesn't know of your interest, don't say or do anything about it.
- If you decide not to move toward a relationship, but the other person is aware of your interest, then speak to him privately and make it objective, saying something like *I like you, but this rule (or my values) keeps me from letting this go any further.*
- If you decide a move toward relationship is possible and appropriate and within the rules, keep it thoroughly separate from work. Don't even leave work together. Don't discuss or e-mail anything about the relationship at or around work, at all.

EXAMPLE: EVEN IF YOU'RE MARRIED . . .

It's a good idea to separate your personal life from work, even if you're married to someone you work with. I once worked for a couple who ran a husband-and-wife CPA partnership. They almost never talked about their personal life at work. I spent a year there and I can remember only two personal comments. Once was a time when the husband was going home for lunch and he asked his wife if he should bring anything back with him. The other was when the husband was being unusually moody and his wife told me that he always had difficulty at that time of year because it was when his mother had passed away.

The lesson: Keep the personal and professional separate, and everyone will be more comfortable and more productive.

You've Broken Up—but You Still Have to Work Together

This may be a problem for two people on your team or for you and someone you work with. A personal relationship has ended, but work life goes on. Both people will have feelings—sadness, loss, hurt, or anger—perhaps each time they see the other person.

You've broken up, but you still have to work together. We're all part of the same team is the place to start. Help the team member see the other person as part of the team, instead of part of a personal problem. And help him focus on the work to be done.

Consider structural solutions as well. Perhaps the two people should see each other only with someone else present. Or perhaps a change of work arrangements can help both be productive while they see less of each other at the office.

Calling Bad Plays—the Line Between Jokes and Sexual Harassment

One person's good joke is another's basis for a sexual harassment lawsuit. In addition to the different personality types, which affect how people hear what is said to them, we also have differences of age and cultural background. A clothing style—such as the bare midriff that has become popular in the last few years—is just an ordinary way of dressing to some people and a sexual come-on to others. As managers, we may find we have to set guidelines for the tone and style that are acceptable at work.

That doesn't play well at the office is a good, inoffensive introduction of the issue. Be sure you are alone with the person, so that you don't embarrass him or her in front of the team. Be sure to focus on perception, not meaning. If the team member protests that what he is saying or doing is harmless, you can reply, *"I know, but at the office we need to be concerned about how people understand us, not just what we mean to say."* A stronger version might be *If that isn't what you meant, then find another way to say it.*

Sexual Politics—Office Power Plays

Sex and power are a bad mix—almost as bad as drinking and driving. At work, there are many chances to give people opportunities, many choices that imply power over what others can and cannot do and what they can make of their lives.

And people are sexual beings: from our style and clothing to our innuendos and jokes, to what we actually do, we send out sexual messages. And when messages about power and messages about sex get crossed, it's an accident waiting to happen.

If you see someone making a decision based on what might be a shaky reason, perhaps related to sexual preference or prejudice, say, *"Give me a good business reason."* For example, perhaps people in a classically female job—such as a typing pool—don't want a man working with them. Say, *"Give me a good business reason why he shouldn't work with you."*

Gender Preferences and Prejudices

We all have preferences—some people are attracted to men or to women, some to people of a certain age or look or style. Many of us also have prejudices—thoughts about what other people should and shouldn't like, should and shouldn't do, should and shouldn't be. Feelings will come up around our preferences and prejudices. But they shouldn't interfere with work. *We're a team: we work together and we leave our likes and dislikes at home* is a good reminder for everyone.

If styles and biases keep coming into conflict, bring the team together for a brainstorming session. Tell the team that you want them to create some ground rules for how we will work together. Ask each person to name one way they don't like to be treated. Ask each of them, in a second round, to name one way they do want to be treated. From this, create a list beginning with the magic words, "We will." For example:

We will:

- Listen to one another with respect.
- Not interrupt each other.
- Ask permission before touching one another.
- Arrive on time for meetings.
- Not raise our voices.

We can think of this as a code of conduct created by the team, for the team. And we can add, *"We will do our best to keep this code of conduct and gently remind one another to do the same."*

Signs of a Hostile Environment

As managers, we should be aware of some very odd legal rules and precedents around sexual harassment. A person who files a complaint of sexual harassment can charge either the individual or the company or both. Key to the question of whether the company is liable for the actions of one employee is the notion of a *hostile environment.* The lawyers for the complainant can look at anything in your company and see if it appears to be a sign of a hostile environment. The suggestive postcard on the bulletin board, the sexually explicit pictures downloaded from the Internet by a team member without your knowledge, even the e-mail full of jokes sent by a friend—all these can be interpreted as signs that an offices allows or supports sexual harassment and should be held liable for the actions of its employees.

At the same time, we don't want to become police. As managers, we should:

- *Lead by example.* So, if you receive an e-mail with inappropriate jokes, don't just delete it. Instead, go to the source and ask them not to send you this kind of thing.
- *Inform others and ask for their support.* If there are corporate rules, let everyone know what they are. If there is sensitivity training, let the team know you take it seriously and you expect them to do so, as well. (Don't just figure it is one more waste of time to comply with regulations.) And if there are no rules, ask the team to work with you to create a healthy work environment and protect the company from trouble.

Chapter 6
When Personal Issues
Affect Work Life

Sometimes, people's home lives—whether physical, emotional, family, or personal—get in the way at work. All of a sudden, a manager has to talk to employees about the very thing we don't know how to say to our own children. Embarrassing as it is, it's our job. And it takes a light hand to do it right.

From Body Odor to Bad Breath

Sometimes, something about a person's physical appearance or smell is offensive to other team members. This situation is fraught with complications. If possible, work with the other team members rather than the person they say has the problem. Ask, *"Could you learn to live with this?"* Talk with them about inoffensive actions they can take or changes to the way work can be done that might eliminate their discomfort.

If their answer is no, you will need to talk to the person whose smell or appearance is disturbing others. Here are some of the complications.

- The person may deny it is a problem and be offended that you are raising it.
- The person may be unaware of the problem and it may be difficult to convince him to take it seriously.
- The person may know about the problem, but not be able to do anything about it.
- The problem may be related to a medical condition. Learning of an employee's medical condition raises additional difficulties. Please be sure to read Chapter 20, When to Get Help.

When you do approach the team member, be circumspect. *A situation has come up affecting team performance, and the others have asked me to talk to you about it. I'm a bit embarrassed because it's kind of personal. Can I tell you what it is?* Then describe the experience other team members are having. Ask if the team member is aware of the issue and how it affects others. Then listen. Be sure to thank the team member for being willing to talk about it and to take whatever steps there might be toward a solution.

EXAMPLE: IT'S GOTTA BE THE HAIR

An HR executive received several complaints from a number of team members that a young manager was "arrogant." When she interviewed him about it, she thought he was a kind and considerate man, but she noticed that he had long hair and he frequently flipped his head back to get it out of his eyes. When he did, he tilted his head a bit and looked—well—arrogant.

She gently told him that his habit was giving the wrong impression. She made a suggestion that no legal department would dare make—that he get a haircut. The man shortened his hair and the complaints vanished.

Story courtesy of Ann F. Romaine

Is Something Wrong at Home?

There are many signs that a team member is unable to focus on work due to stress or problems in his personal life. Some of the most common ones are:

- Showing up late, leaving early, or taking long breaks
- Long, personal conversations on the office phone or cell phone
- A lot of time spent on personal e-mails
- A flood of calls from several people, which can indicate that the team member is trying to coordinate the solution to a problem or handle a crisis
- Changes of mood or temper, indicating stress
- An inability to focus on work or deliver results

Is something wrong at home? can be a good opener. You may want to temper it by first saying, *"You seem to be having trouble focusing on work."* If the team member says everything is fine, then turn the conversation to specific behaviors at work that need more attention or need to change.

If the person says there is a problem, then say, *"I'm sorry that's happening, but I'm glad to know about it."* Find an appropriate way to coordinate a solution—maybe comp time, so that he can take care of the home situation and still get work done. If your company offers sources of support or counseling, be sure to direct the employee to them. (If you're not sure, take the time to find out; your team member will appreciate it.) Often, though, a little flexibility and a good ear are all the help a person needs to bring things under control.

Personal Calls and E-Mails on Office Time

Sometimes, team members spend too much time on personal matters—family, home life, romance, or other business—during work time. When interruptions take too long or happen too often, they really cut into productivity. Studies show that people get only one third as much work done when they are interruptible as when they are not.

Different companies have different attitudes and rules in relation to personal activities during work time. Make sure your team knows the rules and knows if they are flexible or not. Also, the more you know, the better. When you tell team members the rules, also ask them to tell you of events or situations that might demand extra personal time when they first come up, so that you know what is going on.

Everyone goes through busy or chaotic times. Sometimes, there is no avoiding an interruption at work—such as when a child, parent, or other dependent falls suddenly ill or is injured. Other times, there is just too much to do—and some of it has to happen during work time. I know what that's like—I just bought a house and I had to make up time at work in the evenings because some of the phone calls and meetings about the mortgage and inspections had to be during the day. A flexible company will have an easier time retaining good employees, but clear limits are as important as flexibility.

I see you need some time for this. How do you want to balance that with your workload? is a good way to open the issue. Give the employee the responsibility for coming up with a solution and let him know that what matters is good work being done. If the situation is getting out of hand, name specific things the employee must do or complete, with delivery dates. Then say, *"You need to focus on work when you're here. How can we work this out?"* Sit down together, write up a solution—whether it's a limit on the number of phone calls, an arrangement for comp time or evening work, or whatever—and then ask the team member to be as responsible in his job as with the other parts of his life.

Selfish Cell-Phoning

Companies used to be able to control employee time on personal calls by restricting use of the company phones for personal use. Now that most people have cell phones, that doesn't work any more. Using cell phones—or even carrying them—at work can lead to a number of problems.

- Too much work time is spent on personal topics.
- When people are interruptible, they are only one third as efficient as when they do not allow interruptions. Having a cell phone turned on reduces productivity.
- People walking around talking on cell phones or using them in cubicles disturbs others and allows them to hear personal conversations.
- Cell phone ringers disturb other workers, especially in meetings.
- Even carrying a cell phone—especially if it has a camera—must be prohibited in certain areas, such as secure facilities and some courtrooms.
- Cell phones blur the line between home and work and can become major time-wasters.

People may not realize how much time they are spending not working because they are taking or making cell phone calls. If you see a problem, you can say, *"It's easy to spend a lot of time on a cell phone. Have you noticed if it's cutting into your work?"* Then explain that the whole team needs to focus on work during work hours. If the employee is cooperative, a little awareness is probably all that is needed.

Side Jobs on Office Time

What do you do if you discover an employee is working a second job or doing side work for pay from the office?

This is a clear violation of corporate boundaries. Tell the team member, *"You can't mix your business with our business."* Then make the limits very clear: no other business should be conducted while at the office, even using a personal cell phone or e-mail account—time at this job is for this job and company resources and tools are for company purposes only. Even if you allow employees, say, to make photocopies for a child's school event or a charity fundraiser, explain that you don't fund other businesses from your business.

Occasionally, a team member may have a legitimate side business done at a separate time and receive rare calls that he needs to handle. If this happens, tell the employee to answer the phone saying, "I'm at my other job right now" or "I'm at work right now, can I call you back?" Then, keep the calls to under two minutes and use break times or lunch to reply to the call and not from the office.

Selling Stuff to Our Staff

This is one step worse than a side job on office time. Now, the employee is trying to turn team members into his own customers. Often, this begins innocently. The team member might have gotten involved with a network marketing program and been encouraged to sell to people he knows. Or he might see it as a useful and helpful thing to do. The problem is that it often becomes complicated. If another team member is unhappy with a product or service, it can ruin a work relationship. If the program involves upselling or getting others involved as salespeople, the whole situation can get out of control.

You can't mix your business with our business is a good place to start. *Don't sell to other team members.* Explain that if he wants to spend time with team members outside office hours and not at the office, whatever he does there is within his rights, as long as it doesn't interfere with work. Explain the kinds of problems that can happen for the team, even when everyone means well, so that he understands your business reason.

Job Hunting on the Job

What do you do if you find out that a team member is looking for a new job—on company time? There are a few situations where that is reasonable:

- If team members have already been notified of layoffs or of the company closing, allowing some time at work for job hunting is appropriate.
- Some companies, when closing divisions or laying people off, even offer job reassignment assistance.
- If an employee is in a temporary position with a definite end date, then let him know what is appropriate.
- Occasionally, team members may receive unsolicited calls from headhunters at work. Be sure not to blame an employee if he did not initiate the inquiry about the job.

Discovering an employee is looking for other work is a dicey situation. You need to deal with two facts: the employee wants to leave and he is doing something inappropriate in looking for work from his current job. You will have to consider how important it is to keep this team member, plan what you can offer and what you have to say, and then talk with him.

Say, *"Tell me if I'm wrong, but it looks like you're thinking about changing jobs."* Listen to his reply. If you want very much to keep the team member, follow this up with *I'd like to talk to you about what we can do to keep you here.* If you are more concerned about the employee using work time for work, then say, *"I understand you may need to look for other work, but we need to keep that separate from this job."* Then work out the specifics.

Late Arrivals, Extra Breaks

When employees persistently arrive late, take extra breaks or extra long lunch hours, or simply leave early, sometimes we want to yell, "Show up and stay at work." Clearly, that isn't the most emotionally intelligent response.

Instead, try *We need to talk about your work hours.* Then ask, *"What's happening that you're arriving late (or leaving early, or taking extra breaks, or extending lunch hours)?"* Give the team member a chance to explain. Then take your turn and explain to him the effect on his productivity and also on fairness to the team. Come up with an agreement now and a way of measuring his efforts and enforcing the agreement.

If the problem persists, tell him clearly what the consequences will be.

Be careful if the employee's story keeps changing. This can be either a sign of a serious instability in the person's home life or a sign of a serious problem, such as addiction to alcohol or drugs. If you don't think the employee is being honest and making a serious effort to meet work responsibilities, see Chapter 20, When to Get Help.

Chapter 7
Pranks, Put-Downs, and Bending the Rules

A bit of fun at the office is a good thing, but it can get out of hand. How we handle pranks, put-downs, and people bending the rules can establish a workplace that not only is safe, but also feels safe—and that is key to productivity. Why? Because when we don't feel safe, we cannot focus. When we don't feel safe, we're always watching our backs. Without focus, we can't do good work and solve problems.

At the same time, healthy fun is important. If we are too strict, our team will dry up. Creating good office fun and games can bring a team together. It builds trust and develops team problem-solving skills.

From an emotional intelligence perspective, the need to play games and tease others comes from our own emotions. When we are not aware of how we feel, we act out—reacting to our feelings in ways that may be inappropriate. When we learn to be aware of our feelings—and we stop and breathe—we give ourselves options. We can examine our feelings and find out what we really want to say. Then we can find a constructive way to get our ideas across. The best thing we can do for our teams is to practice emotional intelligence—maturity—and model it for our teams.

Act Your Age!

Sometimes, when we see members of our team fooling around, we want to yell, "Act your age!" Well, that would be kind of childish, now wouldn't it? If we feel that impulse, it is best to stop, breathe, and reflect. What's really going on?

- Is it a harmless bit of fun at a moment when we are taking work—or ourselves—too seriously?
- Is it really getting in the way of work?
- Is it really dangerous—such as a prank that could lead to physical injury?
- Is it something that might be OK, but might also cause hurt feelings, tension, or conflict?

Once you clarify your own perspective, you will also want to check in with team members—both those who are doing the pranks or put-downs and those on the receiving end. All perspectives matter—safety, productivity, your view, the perpetrators' view, and the recipients' view. Once you fully understand the situation, use the relevant case in this chapter as a guide for what to say.

Pranks

If you see a prank or practical joke taking place or if someone complains about one, be sure to do these things:

- **Don't participate.** People are likely to feel threatened if a person with authority participates in a joke on them.
- **Make sure it's safe.** If there is any risk of physical injury—however remote—stop the activity and take appropriate disciplinary action.
- **Make sure it won't hurt any feelings.** Think about the target of the joke and ask what the risks are. If it has already happened, take time to listen to the target and hear and respond to his or her feelings.
- **Make sure it won't interfere with productivity.** Sure, the food fight was fun, but who'll clean up the mess?
- **Make sure it isn't part of a pattern of bullying.** Be aware of—and beware of—mobbing, as discussed below.
- **Ask why.** Talk to the perpetrator and satisfy yourself that it was all in good fun and not a sign of resentment or other feelings that could lead to future problems.

The key is to focus on actual consequences with respect to health, safety, and productivity. Remember, though, that includes emotional health and safety. Don't let pranks get in the way of building and maintaining a good team.

Put-Downs

How much does a negative comment—a put-down—matter? First of all, if it comes from you or from another superior to a subordinate and it comes in the presence of others, it always matters. Everyone has a deep-seated fear of being rejected by authority and cast out from the group. In general, I believe that most psychological issues are personal and individual. But this one appears to be truly universal—for all people and for all animals that live in social groups or communities, such as apes, monkeys, and wolves. At some very deep level, criticism by authority can lead to rejection from the group—which leads to death. If that fear response is triggered, it will hurt productivity and teamwork.

What about criticism among members of the team? What is the line where innocent expressions of cultural and personal style become causes of emotional damage?

Unfortunately, there is no one line. The line is in each person's mind, so we must talk to both the perpetrator and the target of the incident. If both are OK with it and the team is OK with it, then let it be. But if it comes from an unresolved issue or it leaves anyone uncomfortable, then teach and model effective, upbeat communication. Here are some key points:

- *Use mirroring.* Most of us feel hurt when we are not heard. We get reactive when we feel that people are not listening to us, not taking us seriously. So model mirroring, the process of repeating someone's ideas back to him or her in your own words, and teach your team to do it as well. You can often begin by saying, "Let me make sure I got this right. You're saying ...."

- *Say, "Yes, and ..." instead of "No, but ...."* In almost all conversation, "Yes, and ..." will carry the same meaning as "No, but ...," but is less critical and argumentative.

- *Use "we."* Don't let the team—or the company—become a "they." Also, instead of saying, "You should ...," we can say, "We'll do better if we ...."

- *Consider what you say.* Instead of opening up our mouths only to insert our foot, we can take a look at what we want to say before we say it. It can help to ask three questions about each thing we plan to say: *Is it true? Is it kind? Is it helpful?*

- *Mean what you say.* Just changing words—from "No, but" to "Yes, and" or any other change—will sound insincere. Reflect on the ideas behind these changes. Shift your stance so that you genuinely want to be inclusive and supportive.

EXAMPLE: BRAINSTORMING—OR BASHING?

One time, I was teaching a workshop on teamwork methods to a very bright group of computer genetics experts. A woman brought up an idea and I suggested we brainstorm ways to make the idea better. The group immediately poured out a barrage of criticisms and challenges.

When they stopped, I asked, "Is that how you brainstorm here?"

They answered, "Yes, always."

I answered, "If it works for you, great. But it actually sounded like you were ganging up and attacking her thinking personally, instead of addressing her idea. Let's try it again, with some different ground rules."

I introduced the ideas presented earlier in this chapter and we continued brainstorming. We got the same good ideas in a much gentler way.

Does that matter? It depends. If everyone on the team is used to a hard style, then it can work. But I've seen some companies that took that approach and thought they were doing well. Then they realized that they were losing good ideas—and, in the long run, losing good people—because their style didn't do enough to respect people while critiquing their ideas.

The lesson: a gentle style is inclusive of people who are quieter. When we create an environment with a challenging style, we may lose their input and, after a time, lose good people from the team.

Tit for Tat

Sometimes, two people on a team play off one another in an escalating cycle of pranks or criticisms. If this ends in laughter and appreciation, it can be part of a healthy cycle of relationship. However, if it goes on without ending or to the point where the team is thrown off balance or where one person wants it to stop and can't, then it becomes a business issue. What was just fun now interferes with the cooperative side of teamwork.

In addressing this with the two people, the challenge is to get both of them to jump out of their own perspectives and see its consequences for the team. It is probably best to talk with each person separately. Depending on the situation, you can open with one of these lines:

- *"I know you think it's all in fun, but the games between you and [other person] have started to hurt him. I'm sure you don't want that. Can we talk about how you can set some limits?"*
- *"The two of you are having fun, but I don't think you understand how other people on the team are feeling. For them, it's threatening."*
- *"You seem to be having fun, but it's taking up a lot of time. How can you trim your sails and steer a course toward a little more work?"*

Bullying and Ganging Up on an Employee

Bullying, or mobbing in the workplace, is a serious problem that costs American business billions of dollars a year. Even if no other type of discrimination—such as racism, sexism, or ageism—is involved, any time a whole office appears to be targeting one person, it is a serious danger sign. Usually, there will be one target, one perpetrator, and a number of others who participate—more or less willingly—and others who turn a blind eye.

The damage—to the person, the whole team, and the company—is much too great for you to turn a blind eye yourself. If you do, corporate management can be seen as condoning, participating in, or even causing the mobbing. When we do that, we're shooting ourselves—and our bottom line—in the foot.

Sometimes, you may find that you have to take a stand against mobbing even when the company is letting it happen. Higher executives may offer excuses, such as "We brought in a new broom to sweep clean, and he's sweeping," or "It can't be that bad."

If you find that your company doesn't help you fight mobbing, then be sure to get a copy of *Mobbing*—see the sidebar for how to order it—and raise the issue clearly at the highest level that you can.

For instructions on how to stop mobbing early, see the situation "Nobody Likes the New Kid on the Block" in Chapter 8, New Employee Orientation Issues.

BACKGROUND: MORE ON MOBBING

Here are some key things that every manager should know about mobbing:

- **Anyone can be mobbed.** The target of mobbing may not be new to the company. People with many years on the job have been mobbed. People at any level—team members, technical staff, managers, even senior executives—can become targets of mobbing.

- **Mobbing can start anywhere.** A boss, a teammate, or even an underling can start the mobbing process.

- **Mobbing happens only if a company lets it happen.** Companies allow mobbing through lack of knowledge—the belief that it can't happen—or through lack of concern. Companies also support mobbing. If we use the company's authority to insist on fairness, we can prevent mobbing.

- **Mobbing hurts the bottom line.** A company where mobbing occurs is not a good place to work, even for those who do it. Mobbing lowers morale and productivity and helps maintain a culture of dishonesty and blame.

- **You can learn more about mobbing.** You can start by reading *Mobbing: Emotional Abuse in the American Workplace,* by Noa Davenport, Ruth Distler Schwartz, and Gail Pursell Elliott (Ames, IA: Civil Society Publishing, 1999), www.mobbing-usa.com.

Time for a Bit of Fun in the Office

A team should have fun more than once a year. In my company, we have Friday Fun every week. Since we're a virtual team—living all across the country—we do it by collecting jokes or making fun of our clients or ourselves on a Web page. We play around, get a bit foolish, and blow off a little steam. We find it actually makes getting back to work easier.

There's a technique in Barbara Sher's book, *Wishcraft* (New York: Ballantine Books, 2004, 2nd edition), called "The Power of Negative Thinking," that can be adapted for a bit of productive team fun. In a team meeting, let one person get up and give a two-minute standup comedy routine about all the reasons that he hates his work—why the work is stupid, ridiculous, and useless. The person can get out all of the team's negative thoughts in a loud, fun, even obnoxious way and receive applause for it. Then, after it's over, go around and have each person express some real appreciation for the team, the boss, the client—whoever got raked over the coals in the comedy routine. Try it—you might just find it makes it easier to focus on the less fun parts of our jobs.

Chapter 8
New Employee
Orientation Issues

When a new employee arrives, the manager is responsible for something called orientation. Why? Because the employee is disoriented on arrival. A new employee is kind of like Michael Jordan switching from basketball to baseball. Even if the employee is good at what she does, she just doesn't know the rules at this ball field. And it's our job to bring her into the game.

Rules and Assumptions

Every organization has its rules. In larger companies, they are generally written down. In smaller firms, they may be passed on by word-of-mouth. There are minor items, such as how strict the company is about arrival and departure times, and major ones, such as policy on use of illegal drugs. But orientation is about more than learning what the rules are. It is about learning which rules matter most, and why, and how to fit in.

As a manager, be sure to take time to bring the new team member up to speed, not just with the work, but with the unwritten assumptions about how people get along. Either take the time to do it yourself or have an experienced—and mature—team member do some mentoring for the new arrival.

"I want you to fit in easily and get along with everyone" is a good opening line. You can also prevent many orientation problems by making it a team effort. Assign one experienced team member to be a mentor for each new hire. Don't always assign the same person; let different people have a hand in helping with each new employee. Sit down with both of them and encourage an open relationship where they ask questions and answer them freely and clearly, rather than making assumptions.

But I've Always Done It This Way!

A team member may be new to the company, but not new to the business. Or, even if he's new to the business, his own habits from home or school may seem to him like the best way to work. To pick a simple example, the record keeping a company does in accounts payable is a lot more involved than what a person usually does when paying the utility bills at home. But a new employee might not know what needs to be done or why. Bills might get paid, but information—crucial for taxes—might get lost and it might not be noticed for months.

When confronted, the team member might say, "But I've always done it this way."

You reply, *"Yes, I understand, but that way doesn't work here."* Then take time to explain the consequences of doing it the company way vs. his way. Show him why it matters and then walk him through the right way. Whenever you train someone in a procedure, especially when he needs to unlearn a different procedure to learn this one, it is a good idea to do these four steps.

1. Do the task and have him watch you and write his own instructions.
2. Read the instructions off slowly while he does the task.
3. Have him do the task. Watch—and interrupt only if he is making a big mistake. When he is done, compare what he did with the steps and change either the work process or the written instructions, so that the two match.

4. Leave him with the assignment to write up the instructions into a formal standard operating procedure (SOP).

SOPs should be filed, referred to, and periodically checked. Sometimes, people find better ways of doing things, and those should be written down.

EXAMPLE: SOMETIMES, DIFFERENT IS BETTER

Perhaps, when you see a new team member is doing something differently, he has actually come up with a better way to do the work. Or, as the old saying goes, there's more than one way to skin a cat—maybe it just doesn't matter how the job is done. How do you know? Look at the work results and their consequences. If the way the new team member is working doesn't create any problems down the road, let him do it his way. If it actually makes things better, it's time to express some appreciation.

An Employee Trying to Change the Rules

Sometimes, a new team member rushes in and tries to get everyone to do things his or her way. Or he just doesn't follow procedure or guidelines, in spite of repeated reminders. In this situation, orientation isn't working. When a team is oriented, the members all move together, in the same direction. And this team member is pulling off in a different direction. You need to find out why.

Even if you've made things very plain and clear, realize that there might still be misunderstanding. People learn in different ways—some through listening, others through reading, and others through watching what other people do. Perhaps the corporate employee manual is online and the employee isn't really comfortable learning at a computer. Perhaps the employee came from a job where no one took the written manual seriously, because it was years out of date. Perhaps the employee is nervously trying to show he can make things better, in order to be accepted on the new job.

In any case, what is needed is clear communication, starting with good listening. Take the employee aside and set up uninterrupted time to talk. Then say, *"I need to understand what is happening here. Why did you [do or not do whatever it was]?"* Try to draw out the team member and have him speak first. If that doesn't work, try *"OK, I'll tell you how it looks from my side, and then you can tell me yours."*

You can bring a team member onto the same page with you only if you can get onto his page and see how it looks from his side.

Lack of Attention to Detail

Sometimes, a new team member is simply not making sure that the job is done well, that all the details are taken care of. This is not surprising—remember that, until orientation is over, the team member is disoriented. Our first step in this situation is to make sure that the team member understands the consequences of good—and bad—work and has clear examples of each. We should make sure the team member has:

- A clear understanding of the consequences of good and bad work
- An example of good work for comparison
- Examples of bad work for comparison
- Clear instructions on how to do good work
- Skills and training sufficient for the job
- Clear instructions on how to check the work, such as completion checklists

If any of these items are missing, work with the team member to create them. There is no better method of orientation than having a team member write the instructions for his own job. If everything is in place and the team member isn't focused, ask, *"What's getting in the way?"* The team member might have to think about this. It could be environmental—some people can't work with music and others need it. It could be interruptions or nervousness. If the employee isn't sure, tell him, *"Do your work. Watch for what stops you or distracts you. Come tell me, and we'll take care of it."*

If this does not resolve the problem, then there may be something deeper involved—anything from a stressful problem at home, a lack of concern about the job, or a bad fit between employee and job to something more serious, such as a drug problem or a psychological condition. Don't jump to any of these conclusions, but do be aware of the possibilities and take a look at Chapter 10, Attitude Problems, and Chapter 20, When to Get Help.

Caring Too Much

Some new team members care too much. This usually leads in one of three directions:

- Overwork to burnout
- Stress, leading to mistakes
- Too much attention on one part of the job and not enough on others

The last thing you want to do is to make the new team member more anxious. You might lighten up the situation with *"You're doing a great job—too great."* Make sure he takes that in. Let him know his place on the team is secure. Then give some gentle, corrective guidance to fit the situation. Try, as appropriate, *"We want you here for the long haul. Take a break before you fry,"* or *"Relax, and you'll do a better job,"* or *"You do this really well. Could you focus a bit more on these other things?"*

Caring Too Little

Sometimes, a new team member seems just not to care enough to do a good job or to learn the job well. Check carefully to see which of these three things is happening:

- The employee does care, but some other concern or stress is getting in the way.
- The employee comes from a different work environment, where no one cared, and he hasn't caught on to the difference yet.
- The employee genuinely is just not that interested in the job or career.

There is a remedy for each of these, as follows:

- Identify the problem and coach the team member to resolve it with *"Let me help you get this roadblock out of the way."*
- Pair him up with another team member, with *"Work together for a while and see how rewarding it is to get good work done."*
- Accept—at least for now—that you may have an average employee and not a stellar performer.

Motivation is tricky business. The best motivation often isn't a paycheck, but a "thanks, good job." The very best motivations are intrinsic, that is, they come from inside a person. And we can cultivate intrinsic motivation by creating a healthy work environment where we respect people, appreciate them, and recognize and reward good work.

Unwilling to Improve

What do we do when a team member appears unwilling to follow our guidance and bring work up to an acceptable level of quantity or quality? We can't assume the best—or the worst.

Meet with the team member and open the serious tone by saying, *"Results are what matter, and the company needs to see changes in your results."* Set your relationship with the team member by saying, *"I'll help all I can, but success is up to you."*

Outline the situation. Then make time to listen. Perhaps the team member wasn't clear about something, even though you thought you taught him. Or perhaps he feels something is unfair or getting in the way. Even if you think it should be irrelevant or you feel you've heard it before, listen again. Take a problem-and-solution approach to whatever the employee raises. And remember—work with the employee, and don't make him into the problem.

Sit beside the team member and walk through the process and the results that you want, in detail. Ask the team member to describe the process and the results as if he were teaching you to do the job. Make sure everything is clear. And then put it in writing. When you are done, he should have a recipe for good work and a sample of good work so he can check it himself. You may have some action items if there are roadblocks for you to clear out of the way. And there should be a committed delivery date, with times for meetings before and after.

You will need to tell the employee the consequences of successful delivery and of failure to deliver, even if that includes possible termination. If an employee is not clear about consequences, then your decision to terminate the employee can be overturned. Be sure to read Chapter 20, When to Get Help, and to discuss the situation with the appropriate HR and legal resources.

You may also want to review Chapter 1, Facing Your Day. Remember: not every difficult situation can be resolved. Make sure the employee has what it takes and is committed to success. Once all external barriers have been removed, it is up to the team member. And it is up to you to make a clear, objective decision, based on performance, during the probationary period.

End the meeting on a positive note by saying, *"I still believe you can make this work. I'll help all I can, but success is up to you."*

Not Ready, Fire

Sometimes, a new team member jumps in and does something before he is really ready. This can be the result of over-confidence or of underestimating the size or the complexity of the job or the situation. The team can handle damage control. Your job is to help the new team member learn and improve.

"Write yourself a simple set of instructions for next time and let me look at it." This will engage the employee in process improvement. If the employee needs more guidance, say, *"Write down what did work, and how you did it. Then write down what didn't work, and how you would do it next time. If you're not sure on that part, ask me or another team member. We'll help you get it right next time."*

Ready, Fire, Aim

Sometimes, a new team member knows how to do something, but messes it up anyway. Perhaps he did it well the first time and made a mistake the second time around. This is common; I call it the *sophomore effect*, because the sophomore year—the second year—of high school or college is often harder than the first. Why? Because, at first, we know we don't know our way around, so we pay attention. The second time, we think we know the ropes. We're overconfident and we jump too soon. (The source of the word "sophomore" combines the Greek words for "wise" and "foolish.") I call this *Ready, fire, aim*.

Say, *"It looks like you missed the target this time. Next time, try ready, aim, fire, instead. You're learning the job, but you need to take more time to prepare."* Reassure the employee that such mistakes are normal early in the job: everyone goes through them and then improves. Explain that it takes experience to know everything that needs to be done and everything that can go wrong. Encourage a little more forethought and let the team member know you want him to get out there and try again.

Not Getting Things Right

What do you do when a new team member has been given clear instructions and an opportunity—over weeks or months—to improve and the work isn't getting any better? If your company has a probationary period for new hires, then it is essential that this be resolved by the end of that time.

The first step is to make an evaluation: over the long term, is the employee's work unacceptable or acceptable? You have to ask this based on the idea that the quality of work may never improve or at least not for a long time. In making this decision, focus on definable, measurable results. The focus is on three options: making the improvement happen, adjusting the job downwards to meet the employee's skill level, or replacing the employee.

The best tools are gap analysis and gap reconciliation. Say, *"Here is where you are now. Here is where you need to be by this date."* Be specific. Make a bulleted list of required results, each an action item with a deadline. Make the team member squarely responsible for the results. Then say, *"We'll help any way we can, but you need to take the lead here. Is there anything you need to do this?"*

Go on to discuss the consequences of failure, such as reassignment or job termination, and then the consequences of success. Reassure the team member that you really do want everything to work out and you still believe that it can work, that he can become a productive part of the team. End with *"You need to make this happen. I think you can."*

Nobody Likes the New Kid on the Block

Sometimes, the current team members don't accept the newcomer. We need to be very careful to see if this is happening. If the whole team seems to agree that the new person isn't fitting in, then you probably aren't hearing everyone's opinion, you're probably hearing only one viewpoint—that of an outspoken opinion leader in the group—and the rest of the team just kind of goes along. A person with an agenda—a hurt ego, or a problem with the new person, or a desire to prove himself—can convince a team to turn against one employee all too easily. This is called *mobbing*, as explained in Chapter 7, Pranks, Put-Downs, and Bending the Rules, and it's kind of like an allergic reaction—the team decides to kick out one person exactly the way a person's body can decide that a new kidney or heart after a transplant doesn't belong and rejects it. The problem is that, just as the new organ is good for the body, so the new team member would be good for the team if we can get the team to accept him.

This kind of bullying can only be stopped if it is caught early. It is even better if we can prevent it. Here are some things we can do to prevent bullying and mobbing:

- Define each job with clear, objective criteria, so that subjective opinions can't be used to drive a person out.
- Create a work environment where respect for the team and cooperation toward team results are expected and rewarded.
- Create an environment that supports honest and open communication, free of blame.

- Communicate changes clearly and include all team members—new and old—equally.

If mobbing does start, we need to catch it early. Once the whole team is set against someone, it will be very hard to keep that person and help the team members see their errors. So, watch for these early signs:

- Many problems are being blamed on one individual.
- One person is being ostracized or isolated.
- An employee's performance drops below what you know he can do and no one offers to help.

If any of these happen, take a firm stand. *"It's our job to make the team work—that includes everyone. Each of us is responsible for helping everyone do a good job and for getting along."* Involve each team member by telling each one, *"Name one specific thing you can do to help [new team member] get along better or do better work."* Make it clear that kicking someone out is not an option, at least not until the other team members have helped all they can and the person has been demonstrated to be incompetent in a supportive environment. *"If you want him to leave, you're going to have to help him stay until we see that, even with all the support we give him, he can't do the job."* To learn more about mobbing, see Chapter 7, Pranks, Put-Downs, and Bending the Rules.

Just Not Fitting In

What do we do when a new employee is doing good work, but just not fitting in on the team?

First, we should realize that, with any new person coming on board, things will be different. We begin by asking ourselves and the team, *"Are things worse—or just different?"*

If things are worse, then we need a specific list of problems—ways that poor communication or poor attitude is really getting in the way of work. Then we can ask the team—the whole team, including the new member—for concrete steps toward a solution.

But, if there is no problem, we need to make room for—and even reward—diversity. I've seen effective teams of stay-late workaholics with one family man who always left at five to be with his family and teams of dedicated family people who appreciated the one workaholic who would stay late. It is harder to maintain fairness in diversity, because it is harder to know what to reward. But diversity is worth it. When we build a team of diverse people, we increase the effectiveness, flexibility, and creativity of our team.

Chapter 9
Time and Punctuality Issues

Arriving late, leaving early, taking too long at lunch, doing personal tasks at work—employees seem to be very creative finding ways to use work time for anything but work. At the same time, we rarely seem to be focused and creative in doing our work. How do we remind our team that 9-to-5 is for work?

It's 9:30, Where's My Team?

Sometimes, the entire office has lost track of time—and of the basic necessity of showing up for work. Before you talk to anyone, try to see why this has happened. Have the rules been clear? Is the system for flex time too complicated? Is there a reason for the team to be disheartened? Do a gap analysis—be able to say where you are, why you think you're there, and where you want the team to be.

Then bring everyone together and open with *It's time for a fresh start.* Lay out your view of the current situation and the desired goal. Before you share your idea of the cause of the problem, ask for their ideas. They may be on a very different page. And you have to start from where they are to bring everyone together.

Once everyone understands what the company needs, define a specific goal and have the team build a plan to get there. Write it up and meet with the team regularly to keep everyone on track.

"Oops, I Missed the Meeting"

What do you do if a team member misses an important meeting? First, do damage control. Have someone fill in or reschedule the meeting. Then it's time to look at the problem and its source:

- Was it a one-time event, such as forgetting the meeting, oversleeping, or running into an emergency?
- Did the team member call in and let someone know? If not, why not?
- Does this seem to be part of a regular or habitual problem?

If the team member really was blindsided by an emergency and he called in, then say, *"These things happen, it's happened to me, too,"* and let it go. If it was an emergency, but the person didn't call in, say, *"From now on, it's really important to let someone know what to do."* That is, the team member should not just say, "I'm going to miss the meeting." The team member should tell the team how to handle the meeting in his absence.

If missing this meeting is part of a bigger picture, then say, *"Things come up once in a while. But this seems like more than that. Please tell me what's happening."* Describe several incidents and ask if there is an underlying problem. Then help the team member formulate an action plan to solve the problem and show up where he needs to be.

Those Little Latenesses Add Up

Some people think that a few minutes here and there doesn't matter. And, in some offices and some jobs, it doesn't. For some jobs, though, such as being a receptionist, punctuality is essential. For others, we may need to stay a few minutes at the end of the day, to make sure things are wrapped up.

Make sure your team members think about these two things:

- *Does it work for the job?* That is, does the behavior create problems for productivity and customer service?
- *Is it fair?* If one person does something a bit different than everyone else, does that end up being fair to everyone?

Once the team member has seen how his behavior looks from the other side, come to an agreement on what the new policy and behavior should be.

EXAMPLE: FIND THOSE FIVE MINUTES SOMEWHERE

This story comes from a manager of a traditional *Fortune* 100 company. A new team member was consistently, punctually five minutes late. When asked why, he explained that he had two choices of commuter bus: one got him in 10 minutes early and the other five minutes late. The boss showed him how much five minutes a day adds up to in a year—more than 8 hours. So the employee was getting an extra day off no one else got. The manager said, "Take the earlier bus or shave five minutes off lunch or take the later bus home, but find that five minutes somewhere." The team member got the message and got on board.

Long Lunches

When a team member disappears for extra long lunch hours frequently—whether that's several days a week or a couple days a week, week after week—two questions naturally come to mind: "Where's he going?" and "Why isn't he at work?"

Both of these questions, used without judgment, are good diagnostic tools. Either he has something going on more important than work or some kind of fear, stress, or anxiety is keeping him from doing his job. Either way, it is cutting into productivity and it is your right to know what's happening and call for a change in behavior.

If the reason for the long lunch is legitimate, such as visiting an elderly relative who recently moved into a nursing home, then the only problems are that the team member didn't tell you and that a comp-time arrangement needs to be worked out. If a job-related problem is at the root of the long lunches, then help the employee resolve it. But be aware that the employee may be caught in an addiction or have some other serious issue to work out. So, approach with clarity and compassion.

We need to talk about your long lunch hours and their effect on productivity is a good opening. And do your best to make it a good talk by listening and letting the employee lead the conversation. For example, if the employee is going for a long exercise walk while thinking about work and is a top performer, maybe you should buy a pair of good walking shoes for everyone on the team.

It's Five O'Clock Somewhere—but Not Here

The line *It's five o'clock somewhere* comes from a country song about a man, depressed about his job, drinking at lunch and not going back to work. Now, in some work environments, dropping half a day for a good reason is just fine. My own company does intense projects and I'll take the whole team out to celebrate at 2 p.m. after a big success. But when an employee has solo dates with the bottle and is AWOL (absent without leave) from work or returns to work unfit to get work done—that is a serious problem.

The next day, take the employee aside and say, *"It's five o'clock somewhere, but not here. What happened yesterday?"* Don't allow the team member to skirt around the issue. If he can't solve the problem himself, he needs help.

Erratic Absences

When a team member is unavailable unexpectedly—losing a half-day or a day of work here or there—over a period of time, it cuts into productivity. There may be a good reason. The team member may have a health problem or may be caring for a chronically ill child, parent, or elderly family member. Sometimes, situations creep up on people and they don't see how bad it is until you point it out to them.

On the other hand, the same behavior can be a sign of more difficult issues, including an addiction problem in the team member, a family member, or a friend who depends on him. Be aware of behavioral addictions, such as gambling, as well as substance addictions.

The key question is: Can you trust the team member to be honest and to try to take good care of work responsibilities? If so, be appropriately flexible and supportive. On the other hand, if you are uncertain of the team member's honesty or commitment, be firm for the sake of the company. Define a required change of behavior with a deadline.

This can get complicated. Be sure to read the section on employee health problems in Chapter 20, When to Get Help. So, when you approach the employee, say, *"You've been out of work a lot. Should I know what's going on?"* If they say no, then focus on work requirements and consequences. Also let them know about resources that are available from HR. If they decide to open up about the problem, be supportive and clear, but watch for signs of dishonesty. Also encourage the employee to talk to HR about health problems that affect work.

We Had Flex Time, but It Broke

Sometimes, an organization's scheduling policy falls apart. The rules about comp time, overtime, and flex time have been forgotten or—more often—time is not being tracked accurately enough to manage the system. If productivity is doing well, it may not matter. But, if productivity is slipping or if people can suddenly announce that they are taking a comp day, then the rules need to be clarified.

Let's start over with our flex time policy is a good place to start. Create a manageable system where time due is written down and reviewed and policies about when it can be taken are clear for everyone. Be sure to come up with a fair way to count flex time that may already be due when you start the new system.

The Same Excuse Every Time

If a person is chronically showing up late or leaving early or disappearing from work and always gives the same reason, one of two things is happening. Either the situation—such as a sick child—is bigger than he's realized or he is not telling the truth.

In the first case, you need to help the team member manage his life so that work works. *"Let me help you think this through"* is a good opening. Define what the job requires and how flexible you can or can't be—and why. Realize that some situations ultimately can't be worked out, but that with people who focus on results rather than rules and want to work together to make it work, a solution that balances life and work can usually be found.

If you find that you don't believe the team member's story, you've come to a difficult place. Say the team member claims illness. Do you really want to treat him like a child by asking for a note from the doctor? Make an effort to re-establish trust, but, if that doesn't happen easily, see Chapter 20, When to Get Help.

A Different Excuse Every Time

Sometimes, a team member comes up with a different excuse every time. Each one may be believable, but, when you put them all together, you realize that this person's life is an unbelievable soap opera. As one manager said about an employee's stories, "How many grandmothers can one man have, that he had to go to all their funerals?"

Unfortunately, individually believable lies are a part of the life of someone with something to hide, such as an addiction. It is hard to be sure without being intrusive. Perhaps we can never be sure. So we have to refocus on the fact that the team member is not doing his job. Simply set a limit of allowable absences—with or without reasons—and watch the team member's work performance and behavior at work closely. If anything seems out of the ordinary, manage the situation with tips from Chapter 20, When to Get Help.

Working Overtime, All the Time

Sometimes, the actual corporate culture is far from the rule-book. Perhaps people normally work 60-70 hours a week. If so, what happens when a new team member signs on and works a regular 40-hour week? Is that a case of not fitting in? Sometimes, but not always. I have seen offices that are a mix of workaholics and family men and women who limit their jobs. Everyone contributes and both individual results and departmental productivity are just fine. We shouldn't allow corporate culture or ideas about how much work people do become more important than productivity—which is a department's bottom line.

Also, one employee or a whole team working long hours might be heroic—or it might be a sign of bad management. I know one *Fortune* 500 company that gives bonuses to project teams that do good work. They used to reward the all-weekend work heroes. Then they realized that they were rewarding bad planning. The real heroes at the company were the teams that completed their projects on time without having to work overtime.

If conflicts arise around this issue, be sure to separate the corporate culture, company rules, and work results. And it's the work results that matter most.

Chapter 10
Attitude Problems

Respect is an essential quality in all relationships. The most basic level of respect is that we treat people as people, as responsible for making their own choices. Then we can help them see the consequences of those choices. We can also respect particular talents and skills, giving us an accurate appreciation of what each team member can do. When we respect a problem, we appreciate what team members *can't* do, when they need extra time or help with a problem, or when the team needs to call in outside expertise.

It is also important to respect ourselves, our skills, and our limitations. A realistic self-assessment empowers us to do what we can and to learn to do what we can't do.

As we respect our team, we model respectful ways of seeing and relating to others. From this basis, we can then intervene—when necessary—when lack of respect within the team gets in the way of good work and a healthy work environment.

Respect for People

What do you do when a team member expresses a basic lack of respect for other people in general? This can take the form of a sarcastic or cynical attitude or it can be a prejudice toward a group of people. Generally, such attitudes have deeper underlying psychological or social roots, but it is not our job to delve into those. It is our job to help every team member participate in a healthy work environment.

The solution is the golden rule: *Act toward others the way you would want them to act toward you.* But you're a manager, not a preacher. So take these steps when talking to the team member:

1. Focus on specific behaviors—word choice, tone of voice, lack of responsiveness.
2. Let the team member know how others react to those behaviors. Gently tell the team member, *"This is what other people have said to me ...."*
3. Ask the team member, *"Is that the response you want from them?"*
4. Usually, the answer will be "no." Then you can say, *"It's your job to communicate effectively—to find a way to say what you mean and give the impression you want to give. Can I help you think that through?"* If the team member agrees, move into a discussion of what the team member really wants to convey, with some role-playing to try things out and see what works.
5. If the team member says, "Yes," to the question in step 3, meaning he wants to push people away, ask

him, *"Why don't you want to get along with the team?"* or *"What's troubling you?"* and follow the discussion where it leads.

6. After the discussion, let other team members know that the team member who was disrespectful is working on it and that they should give him another chance and try to work with him.

Respect for Roles

Sometimes, a team member fails to respect the role of another person—a customer, a boss, an expert, a senior executive. For example, the words "Would you please ...?" mean something very different coming from a team member, where it is a request, and from a senior executive, where it is a polite form of an instruction. In the first case, it might be right to say, "I'm sorry, but I don't have the time." Not in the second.

Where a person should be served—either because he is the customer or because of seniority—then team members need to listen to requests and fulfill them in a spirit of service, unless the request is truly unreasonable. Where a person should be listened to, the team member should learn to listen well, understand, and engage in active, respectful dialog where there is disagreement. For example, it is better to say, "I don't see how that would work," rather than "No, that wouldn't work."

Say to this person, *"As people, we're all equal, but you also have to respect the person's role, experience, and expertise."* There are some other phrases useful in particular situations: *The customer may not always be right, but the customer always has a point,* and *His expertise is worth listening to.*

Who's the Boss?

Sometimes, a person who reports directly to us doesn't respond well to instructions or guidance and we want to yell, "I'm the boss!"

That doesn't work. Instead, take time to ask yourself, *"What about this team member's behavior is bothering me?"* Separate what he is doing from your reaction to it. Then ask, *"Is my reaction reasonable?"*

If it isn't, then there is nothing to say to the team member. Instead, you need to let go of your reaction. If, on the other hand, your reaction is reasonable, then you need to approach the team member. *I want to know how you react when I say ...* is a good place to start. From there, clear away any misunderstandings about what the team member intends. Perhaps he can find a different choice of words or way of responding to you.

It may turn out that there is something more difficult. Perhaps the team member does not feel respected by you or has hurt feelings from some incident. Perhaps there is a major cultural difference getting in the way. If so, say, *"I want to be on the same side with you and work this out. Will you work with me?"* Then take the discussion from there.

Acting Superior to Teammates

Sometimes, one team member—consciously or unconsciously—plays the role of expert or authority on the team. Playing this role—by criticizing people instead of helping them, for instance—doesn't help the team. There are two issues to look at: Does the team member really have something special to offer? What is the source of the attitude?

The answer to the first question is usually yes, because everyone has something special to offer. Give recognition to experience and expertise—and ask other team members to recognize it.

Say to this team member, *"Respect everyone as a person and value the different qualities of people on the team."* Ask the team member, *"How do you feel about people on the team? How do you think they feel about you?"*

If the person is critical of others on the team, thinking that they are incompetent or that they don't know what they should know, say, *"Then help them with your knowledge, instead of criticizing them."*

If the person feels that others are critical of him or that he just doesn't fit in, then say, *"Isolating yourself by acting superior won't help. Work with them and they will work with you."*

One issue lies beneath both problems—acceptance. Help the team member accept himself and accept that this is the team that's here to do the job. From a place of acceptance, we can all help one another.

Always Sparring with Me

Sometimes, a team member takes an attitude toward the person he or she reports to. Psychologists will probably tell you that this is transference, and that the team member has issues with his mother or father but is playing them out with you instead. If these clashes are respectful and lighthearted, we can make room for them. But when they get in the way of good communication and effective work, something needs to change.

I'd like to talk to you about the way we work together is a good opening that puts the two of you on an equal footing. Then discuss how the specific behavior appears to you. Phrases like *When you do this, it seems to me that ...* are useful. Sometimes, it helps to agree on specific phrases to remind us not to get caught up in our reactions or to agree to stop, breathe, and lighten up.

Reassure the team member of your respect and appreciation for him. Ask if there is something that you say or do that puts him on the defensive or makes him feel less appreciated. If he responds, acknowledge the behavior. Try to change it, if you think that is reasonable. If you aren't sure you can change it, reassure the team member by saying something like "When I say [whatever], I'm sorry it sounds that way. What I really mean is [something else], but if I can't remember to say it, I hope that you will remember I didn't mean what you thought I meant."

People are people: habits and attitudes are hard to change. The key is to build a larger relationship and let the sparring be a small part of it that doesn't get in the way.

Always Sparring with Each Other

Sometimes, two team members play off against one another. If this brings out good ideas and gets work done, great. But if either person becomes uncomfortable or threatened, it is time to ask the two to reassess their relationship. Bring them together and ask, *"Could the two of you find a different way to do this?"*

EXAMPLE: MATURITY IS HOW YOU DEAL WITH IMMATURE PEOPLE

In my first managerial position, I had 10 student assistants, many of whom worked well into the evening. One time when I was not at work, I got a call from one of them. He and another team member had nearly gotten into a fistfight. Over the phone, I talked him through the situation to take care of the immediate problem. Later on, I took each of them aside and listened to his side of the story. As each of them told it, the other person had used words and made gestures that provoked an angry response—and they were probably both right.

I said the same thing to each of them: *"Your maturity isn't in how you deal with people who treat you well. It is in how you handle situations where other people are being immature."* Both of them grew up a lot from that experience and contributed more to the team.

Mistreating a Customer

Sometimes, people make big mistakes. If a team member gets angry with a client or says something really embarrassing, it is hard on everyone. But almost no single action—unless it is criminal or results in physical injury—warrants major long-term consequences. The key to good team building and staff development is to allow people to move through their mistakes, learning as they go.

Getting angry with a customer is not the end of the world should be followed by *What can you learn about yourself from this?*

If possible, have the team member apologize to the customer or apologize for the company.

We can take a similar approach if a team member says something offensive to a senior executive. There may be a need to clear things up at both ends. It can be challenging to build relationships with people in senior positions, but it's worth doing, because it gives you the authority to handle situations and keep the team growing.

To the senior executive, send an e-mail saying, *"Let me know if you want to talk about what happened with my team member."* Talk with the team member between sending that message and talking to the executive and clear up the issue in whatever way is best. Then you are ready to speak with the executive. Mostly listen, but you can also say, *"I've already spoken to my team member about this, but if there is more you want him to know, I'll tell him."*

Chapter 11
Problems Between
Generations

Sometimes, age becomes an issue. The Baby Boomers, Gen X, and Gen Y all have different work ethics. While young folks can't get used to office routine, old folks can't adjust to change. You will be old someday. You were young once. A little sympathy will go a long way.

The key is that respect for all people as people comes first and that recognition of age, youth, experience, and status takes second place to that. If we live with this in mind, we teach it by example and we find a team with younger and older workers is a real asset. If we forget that respect for all people comes first, we are in danger of allowing "isms" in ourselves and others to reduce the quality of the work environment and do damage to performance. In addition to the well-known issues of racism, sexism, prejudice by ethnic background, nationality, religion, and sexual preference, we need to be aware of two more. One is ageism—bias for or against older or younger people. The other is rankism, or at least that term is used by author Robert W. Fuller in *Somebodies and Nobodies: Overcoming the Abuse of Rank* (Gabriola Island, BC, Canada: New Society Publishers, 2003).

Understanding rankism and ageism is crucial to you as a manager. Our society needs to recognize rank, expertise, status, and hierarchy. For example, a nurse cannot make the same decisions as a doctor must make and, sometimes, a nurse must follow the instructions of a doctor without questioning them. The challenge is to avoid abuse of that special qualification, rank, or status. For example, hospitals where doctors are trained to work well with nurses experience less staff turnover and are able to provide better patient care at lower cost.

The core of avoiding or resolving these difficult situations is to put respect for all people—for each person as a human being—before consideration of differences. Then we can make room for relevant differences in the workplace while maintaining a civil society and a productive team.

EXCEPTION: FOR SOME BUSINESSES, AGE DOES MATTER

There are some businesses where age does matter—because it matters to the customer. If the company sells products to teens and 20-somethings, then a younger sales force or advertising design crew makes sense. If you work for the AARP (American Association of Retired Persons), then an older customer service team might be more effective.

These, however, are issues related to corporate planning, image, public relations, and hiring. In these cases, it is important to make a distinction between the legitimate business case and general ageism—the bias in our society. For example, in the '60s, some airlines more or less required that "stewardesses" be young, attractive women. That is no longer acceptable (or legal).

Even in a business where age does matter, diversity and experience help. Walt Disney was creating cartoons for children even as an older man. TV shows that target young audiences benefit from experienced—older—crews. And a fresh perspective coming out of recent schooling might be helpful in addressing the problems of elderly customers.

The lesson: our job is to make sure the company benefits from the gifts each employee—young or old—has to offer.

Business: The Last Generation

Sometimes, even though we are managers, we are the new kids on the block. We may join a company or be assigned to a team where people who report to us have been there longer, have more experience, or are older than we are. The first thing we should do is value the gift in each person. Whether we say it aloud or not, we should approach each person who is older or more experienced thinking, *"I appreciate your experience and what it offers the team. I look forward to learning from you as we work together."* If we think it will be well received, it is OK to say this aloud. Remember, though, that specific praise for skill and results is better than general praise. So you might say something like *"You did that really well, and it helped the team get the job done."*

Take the frame of reference of appreciation and respect when you approach problems that might be related to differences of age and experience, such as an older or more experienced team member:

- Being unwilling to learn new methods, tools, or technology
- Not respecting your role as a manager, not listening to your suggestions or directions
- Not appreciating the contributions of younger team members
- Not working well with people who have less experience—not able to "suffer fools gladly."

Before you do anything, make sure that there is a real problem—something that affects performance and work results. Differences of style and ways of working with the team—whether due to age or anything else—are not, in themselves, a problem.

Why is your expression of respect so important? Because, quite often, resistance is a result of feeling inadequate or uncertain about the job. *"Let's discuss this, I really value your contribution"* is a good place to start. You can follow up with whichever of these applies to the situation:

- To overcome resistance to new methods: *"You do good work, and I want you to be able to use this new [computer, tool, method]."* Then listen, seek willingness, and get a very clear sense of what training and practice are necessary to make it work.

- To increase his respect for you: *"and I hope you value my contribution as well. When you [say or do whatever], I think maybe you don't appreciate me or don't welcome me as your manager."* Say how you feel. Then, let the team member respond.

- To increase his appreciation of the contribution of other team members: *"and I want you to appreciate what other team members are doing, too."* Then bring up the specific situation and discuss it. Be aware that the older team member may not realize he has done anything to offend anyone.

- To get him to reconsider a critical attitude toward team members: *"and I really want you to appreciate the work of everyone on the team. Not everyone has your experience. Could you help them, instead of criticizing them?"*

"Things Aren't the Way They Used to Be"

When you hear this complaint from a person with long tenure—in life or on the job—it's time to be lighthearted, but take it seriously. *"You're right; what don't you like about the way things are today?"* is a good opener. Listen, because maybe the team member just needs to complain before accepting the change. And listen, because maybe the voice of experience is telling you something you should know—a good way of doing things that is being lost, a potential problem with the new system, or a change that could really affect productivity or business success.

If you find an issue that needs addressing, you might call the team together to resolve it. Some problems can be seen only by those with experience and be solved only by those with a fresh perspective. You can open the session by saying, *"[team member] sees a situation that might concern all of us. Let's work to understand it and build a solution."*

"I Don't Get No Respect"

This line from the late comedian Rodney Dangerfield points to a problem in our team. Sometimes, people with greater experience or training expect to be treated in a certain way. But, in a diverse culture, other team members may not accord special respect to people with special status. It may be more important to other team members that we are all equal as people.

If a team member complains about a lack of respect from others on the team, take it seriously. The problem could be anything from a bit of friction to the basis for a charge of discrimination. It's important for you to find out what is going on and to respond effectively.

For example, a team member may be accustomed to special treatment. Perhaps he used to have a secretary or an assistant and didn't have to do certain jobs. Perhaps she thinks that the title Director of Research, along with a Ph.D., means that she shouldn't have to take a turn cleaning up the kitchen area. In cases like this, work with the entire team to create a set of ground rules—as described in Chapter 5, When Sex Shows Up at Work—and tell the person, *"In the work that you do, you're special. But, as people working together, we all share the load."*

On the other hand, if the head of research says that she needs to work without interruptions or that her ideas need to be taken seriously at meetings, she has a point. In the first case, some kinds of work really don't go well if the person can be interrupted, so it's a team productivity issue. Even if there is an open-door policy, the one team member may set certain hours when her doors are open and certain hours when they're not. In the second case, some people challenge every idea equally, without considering the source. This can seem disrespectful to trained, experienced team members. They can feel like they're being told to check the basics when, as a habit, they always do. In that case, you might go to the team member who likes to play devil's advocate and say, *"We want your thoughtful criticism. But, if you really want to be valuable to the team, listen and understand before you challenge. Sometimes, it's better to ask, 'Could you explain that to me?' than to say, 'That won't work!'"*

EXAMPLE: NOW, THAT'S EXPERIENCE!

I once interviewed a project manager who headed a team of radio engineers. Their job was to build links across all of Southern California so that the company could keep in touch—one division with another and from headquarters to service crews deployed throughout the region. The project manager had been in the field and with the company for 12 years. His projects were expensive—especially when they went wrong. I asked him what the key to his success was. He replied that, with only 12 years' experience, he was new in the field. He relied on several of his team members—each of whom had been on the job for over 20 years—to provide the experience and technical knowledge to ensure success.

The lesson: just because we are managers, that doesn't mean we know more than our team members. Respect experience, education, and talent on your team. Rely on it. Even allow yourself to be overruled when they're right and you're wrong.

Business: The Next Generation

Sometimes, we have difficulty managing the work of people younger than we are. Our first step should be to check assumptions—maybe we are just not understanding or just not being understood. Create or find real examples of good and bad work, and discuss the business consequences of good work—satisfying customers, meeting quotas, doing what needs to be done. People with less work experience often unconsciously assume that work is like school or that work on this job is like work for another company, perhaps poorly managed.

Begin with *"Let's focus on the job."* Put the job in front of you and the other person—on a table, a board, or a flip chart—and stay on the same side with him. Build a give-and-take and work through the issue together, rather than facing one another. When I face another person directly, he has to face me. And then I—my status as boss, our age—become highly visible and become the issue. Instead, let's stand beside our team members. If we are beside an employee and he is looking at the problem—on the computer screen, in a piece of machinery, or laid out as a plan on a desk or whiteboard—then the personal issues take a back seat and the business issues can be addressed.

Are We Speaking the Same Language?

Sometimes, it seems like the English language changes every 10 years. I remember when a CD was a special kind of savings account from a bank—a certificate of deposit. Now, it's an outmoded way to play music if you haven't gotten an MP3 player yet. On the TV show *The Dead Zone*, Johnny Smith wakes up from a six-year coma to find that George Bush is again president—only it's a different George Bush and Johnny's musical taste is, well, passé.

When misunderstandings like this come up in casual conversations, it's best just to enjoy them. Being open and willing to learn will help your team members drop their defenses.

But sometimes, these misunderstandings make a difference at work. Whether it's engineering, fads, or fashions, we need to understand our customers and make sure our team members understand one another.

When it comes to social matters, I have no problem being clueless. *"I haven't kept up with TV. What's that all about?"* is what I will ask if I think it will help the team. When it comes to engineering issues, I say, *"When I became a manager, I made a decision not to keep up with the latest technology. I can follow your ideas, but I need you to fill me in on the terminology and the details."* Speaking this way, I express two key principles: diversity helps the team and it's good to be honest about what we don't know.

Age and Ageism

Ageism is a type of discrimination and, legally, can be a violation of an employee's civil rights. Most commonly, this refers to discrimination against the elderly. But a claim can be filed by a young person if he or she feels that unfair treatment is due to age.

As managers, it is best to go beyond legal requirements and make sure that a person's age is not an issue in the workplace. We do this in two ways:

- *What's good for one person is good for everyone.* Say that the company offers a program on prevention of heart attack and stroke. You could introduce it by saying, *"This may seem to matter more to some than others. But I want everyone to be healthy, and the sooner we start, the better. What we learn can help us and our families. What we do can help us live longer—but only if we start now. Let's do this as a team."*
- *Do not condone a hostile environment.* Whenever claims of bias and discrimination arise, lawyers can come looking for evidence of a hostile environment. Then you may find you wish you'd known about—and stopped—the circular of e-mail jokes that went around the office talking about an old woman's false teeth. It seemed harmless at the time; now it's used as proof that you allowed these things to slip by, making your company responsible for what one employee did to another. Teach everyone on your team: *"Protect the company and protect your jobs. Be fair and be respectful in*

everything you say and do." If people complain that they can't tell jokes any more, say, *"Life is funny enough without off-color jokes. Just tell us what you did this weekend."*

"I'm Being Sidelined"

If a team member complains of being sidelined—of being excluded or of being given irrelevant work—take this complaint very seriously and investigate it. It can be a sign of ageism and it also can be a sign of mobbing, as discussed in Chapter 7, Pranks, Put-Downs, and Bending the Rules. Even if it is something more minor, such as friction on the team, you should deal with it promptly so that it doesn't reduce self-respect or productivity and doesn't snowball into something worse. Sit down with the employee and ask two questions:

- Tell me what's happening.
- When did this start? How are things different now from the way they were before it started?

Allow the team member to complain, to tell stories, to get it out of his system. Then focus on creating a bulleted list of facts and a table of comparisons. Focus on work items first, such as importance of assignments and inclusion in meetings, but also include social interactions. Inform HR of the situation and ask for guidance, as we discuss in Chapter 20, When to Get Help. At the same time, use your own power and influence to rebalance the situation so that every team member is valued and included, boosting team performance.

EXAMPLE: LITTLE THINGS ADD UP

In my second job out of college, I was sidelined. A series of small actions took place, but the boss justified each one. I was promoted to manager, but given an office across the hall from everyone and told, "We just don't have room over here." An evening workshop was given for the staff by a specialist visiting from Japan and no one told me about it. I wanted to take a long lunch to see the Boston Marathon, but was being so criticized I didn't dare ask for comp time—and the whole office went to the Marathon without me: "Oh, we just forgot to tell you."

Back then, I knew something was wrong. Now, I know I was being mobbed. The company lost a good employee—and I had to do a lot of work to rebuild my self-esteem.

The lesson: be careful not to brush off little things. If you don't turn them around, they add up.

Chapter 12
Justice Issues on the Job

A friend of mine did not receive a promotion and someone else was promoted over him. He went to the boss who made the decision and said, "That wasn't fair." The boss replied, "Life isn't always fair." My friend quit and got a better job. The old company really lost out, because my friend was good at what he did. Why did he leave? Well, he agreed that life isn't always fair. The problem is that the boss denied responsibility. The boss had a chance to make life fair this time and didn't. If his boss had answered differently, perhaps saying, "It isn't fair, but here's why I had to do it," then my friend might have stayed on the job.

We need to own responsibility for our choices and we need to help our team through unfair events, so that they can keep focused on the work at hand. These are part of the larger job— making the work environment as fair as possible in a world that is all too often unfair.

Broken Promises

When a team member feels that a promise has been broken, we need to deal with it. Otherwise, the team member will be left dealing with it alone. Then, he has been let down twice—by the broken promise and also by us and the team. Or, if the team supports him and we don't, then a rift grows between management and workers—between us and our team.

Our question is simple: *What happened?* As we hear the story and then learn about or listen to the other side as well, we should try to work out these facts:

- Is it a case of a clear broken promise or is it a misunderstanding?
- What was the promise? Was it in writing?
- Who made the promise? A team member? Company policy? Someone representing the company? Particularly, how are we involved?

Depending on the situation we find, we should take appropriate action:

- *If a promise was broken and it is in our power to keep it,* then we should keep the promise or we should come as close to that as we reasonably and affordably can and apologize for the gap.
- *If someone else made a clear promise to the team member,* then we should go to the person with or for the team member and ask that person to make good on the promise.

- *If there was a misunderstanding,* then we should get clear on both sides and present both sides as fairly as we can. And we should be willing to go an extra mile one way or another to preserve the relationship between the team member and the company. We should also counsel the team member to get promises in writing and be very careful about future understandings. If the employee is not inclined to be trusting, say, *"I encourage trust, but I also encourage you to make sure everyone understands each other."*

- *If a promise was broken and it can't be made up,* then we need to be as clear as possible about why the situation has happened and what we will do to prevent it from happening again. These types of situations would fall into this category: an employee is promised a raise, but then the company puts in a budget freeze that locks salaries, or an employee is promised a chance to manage a project, but then the project changes and someone else—genuinely more qualified—is selected.

When broken promises arise from communications failures or misunderstandings, this is much easier than when they arise from dishonesty or a genuine lack of integrity—that is, someone who doesn't care about keeping his word. We will look at these more difficult situations later in the chapter.

Seeing the Other Side

Sometimes, a team member will think something is unfair, but that is only because he doesn't see the whole picture. Then you need to say, *"I need you to see the other side of the story. Your side is ...."* Repeat a short form of his own story back to him, so he feels acknowledged and understood. Then, continue by saying, *"From the other side,..."* and explain how it looked and why it had to be done that way. Then work to decide if the situation is resolved or if some change of decision or further action is required.

If two people on your team are having this kind of conflict, you can bring them both together and have them speak with you. Mirror what each one said while the other listens. By standing in the middle and slowing things down, you can often get two people to hear one another and settle their differences. In setting this up, say to each of them, *"Listen to him along with me, and we'll both listen to you, too."*

It's Just Not Fair

When a team member says, "It's just not fair," you know that something has upset him deeply. And it is a wonderfully honest statement. It's also time to slow the situation down.

I hear you is the best place to start. If the team member is very upset or angry, ask him, *"Please slow down and catch your breath."* Then add, *"Let's go through this step by step."* Practice active listening, acknowledging everything you hear without adding anything of your own. Then pull out a piece of paper and say, *"Let's make a picture of this."* Make a bulleted list—or even a diagram—of the actual situation, including all the important points.

If others are involved, now is the time to bring them in and hear all sides of the story. If people are really upset with one another, work with them one at a time before bringing everyone together. Lay out the situation and ask each person, *"Was that fair?"*

If anyone thinks it wasn't fair, then build a team consensus on two points:

- What, if anything, should be done about this situation?
- What should be done to prevent problems like this one in the future?

Make sure the results are written into a memo or policy. This is good team problem solving—you don't want to lose the results.

Chronic Unreliability

When one team member is chronically unreliable, it creates an unfair situation for the whole team in many ways. Other people need to cover for him or make up for his work. Or, if team performance—and compensation—are based on team productivity, then everyone loses due to the poor work habits of one person.

The simple truth is that we have to resolve such situations quickly or good people will leave the team and the company. Whenever we are inclined to give a poor performer another chance, we must realize the risk we are taking in terms of the team and the team's trust in us. Here are some things to keep in mind:

- The sword cuts both ways. If we cut a team member some slack through a difficult time and he pulls through, then everyone will trust you more, because they know that they will get support in the same situation. On the other hand, if we damage team productivity to give a shot to a team member who doesn't pull through, then we've pulled our whole team down.
- The situation is made more difficult if we are privy to confidential information about the poor performer's challenges. The team members will have a hard time trusting us when we can't tell them what is going on.
- The situation is made most difficult if a team member turns out to be lying, caught in an addiction, or engaged in criminal activities. Then, our giving a second chance can make us look very bad.

We will be making a difficult call, probably with incomplete information—and maybe false information—about the underperforming team member's real situation. Here are some things we can do to keep the situation in balance:

- Require small, concrete, measurable steps of improvement. For example, if a team member has been failing to show up for work and has a real need for time off, adjust his schedule, but require that he keep to a planned schedule.
- Set specific deadlines for each improvement. Keep everything in writing—and don't let things slide.
- Get help from HR or other support, as discussed in Chapter 20, When to Get Help.
- Keep the team informed frequently, even if all you can say is "I'm meeting with him twice a week to work out the situation. Please help all you can while we work this out."
- When the situation is over, debrief your team. Let them vent any frustration and tell them anything you've learned from the situation. If the problem leads to any new rules or guidelines, develop them with the team, if possible, and certainly make sure the whole team knows what they are.

Chronic Complaining

Some team members are chronic complainers. Unfortunately, when we're children, some of us discover that complaining works to get us what we want, so it becomes a habit. If the complaining is light and joking—if no one is put down by it—and if it doesn't interfere with work, then we can let it slide and make room for people to be themselves. But if the complaining is causing the team to lose focus, or draining energy for work, or being used to manipulate work, then we need to ask for change. There are two kinds of complaining; we need to deal with each one differently.

If a team member is complaining to get his way—to make someone else do the work or to get the team to do things his way—then we need to say, *"Complaining isn't an effective way to ask for what you want."* Let all team members know they're responsible for effective communication with the team and that complaining doesn't move things forward. Everyone needs to look at problems and work together to come up with solutions. If you need to, explain to the complainer how he sounds to others and that if he has a legitimate concern, the team will help come up with a way to address it.

The other habit of chronic complaining is where people complain about things that we can't change. The best response to that is *Let's focus on what we can do and where we can make a difference.* Teach people to empower themselves by focusing on the contribution they can make, not the many things we can't change, but wish we could.

Blaming Others for Our Mistakes

Some team members may blame others for their own mistakes, in either obvious ways or subtle ways. When people do this, they position themselves as victims and contribute much less than they might. Say, *"We empower ourselves only by taking responsibility for our own choices."* An even stronger statement might be *"If you own what you did, you can learn from the consequences."* Then share a story of a time you made a mistake and owned it and what you learned.

EXAMPLE: I WROTE THE CHECK

About 12 years ago, I lent a friend some money to keep his business going until he could release his new product. He was sure he could pay me back as soon as the product was released. Well, to make a long story short, he was fooling himself. I lost a lot of money—and I'd be fooling myself if I said I didn't get angry. But I got over it. Because, when I looked closely at the situation, I saw one thing: whatever he did or didn't do, I wrote the check.

Now, every time someone makes a mistake and I start to get angry, I look at the situation and see how I got involved and what I did. And I say to myself, *"I wrote the check."*

I don't want to get angry with myself. I'm part of the problem—that is, some decision of mine involved me in the situation. I remember my part and very rarely get angry any more. Instead, I get ahead by learning something and changing what I do.

Unacknowledged Integrity

So far, we've talked about dishonesty and lack of integrity. But, to be fair, we also have to recognize the good in our team. Unfortunately, all too often, the squeaky wheel gets the grease. While we are running around dealing with difficult situations, several people on our team have their shoulders to the wheel and are doing good work, sometimes even in the face of difficult situations.

It is essential that we acknowledge them. Have weekly staff meetings and use them to appreciate doing routine work, meeting deadlines, and taking good care of what needs to be done. When people say, "I was just doing my job," I reply, "*I appreciate people doing their job, because, in this world, that's pretty rare.*"

Chapter 13
Anger on the Job

When anger shows up in the office, it's frightening—and it can be contagious, too. As managers, it is part of our job to create an environment where workers are safe and feel safe. At the same time, we don't want to lose an employee to one angry outburst, because people can change and they should have a chance. Learning to judge anger and work for change while keeping the office safe is an important—and difficult—job.

One Angry Outburst

If a team member who doesn't usually get angry gets angry just once, it is important to take care of the incident and everyone involved to maintain the integrity of the team. With the person who got angry, find out why and how he feels about it. He is likely to feel apologetic or ashamed. Make sure that the underlying issue is resolved and ask him to separate the issue from his feelings, apologizing with a line such as *The issue was troubling to me, but I'm sorry, I shouldn't have gotten angry the way I did.*

Also talk with whoever received the brunt of the anger and anyone who saw the incident, to make sure that they are OK with it.

Chronic Anger

Some people—and I used to be one of them—carry anger around with them, either as a low-level irritation at everything or as a tendency to raise their voices too often. When a team member has these habits, it can throw the whole team off balance. An angry style can have many sources, including:

- The habits the person learned as a child from family and culture
- Stresses in life, including unfair situations and things we want to change that we can't change
- Fear of not being accepted
- Physical health issues, such as chronic pain, that reduce our ability to cope with stress

To participate on a team, a person with a tendency toward anger must become aware of it and bring it under control. He or she needs to establish certain absolute limits—such as never threatening to hit anyone and never breaking anything—and also to find ways to deal with the anger and manage his behavior, such as walking away from difficult situations and knowing when to use e-mail rather than get into a conversation that might turn difficult.

If you see a team member getting angry more often, ask about it. *Are you under more stress lately?* is a good opener. Then you can introduce a specific incident, saying, *"I noticed that you ..."* or *"A team member got scared when you ...."* But don't let the conversation get stuck on a single event. Instead, move to the general issue of how the team member will become aware of and manage his behavior from now on.

To keep it from being demeaning or overly psychological, you can talk about professionalism, rather than maturity, and about stress, rather than anger.

Signs of Serious Danger

Everyone deserves a safe working environment—and that means an environment that feels safe, as well as being safe. An employee who engages any of the following behaviors creates a threatening environment for the team.

- hits or throws something at someone in the office
- brings a weapon to work or brandishes anything as a weapon
- threatens to hurt someone (if the person who was threatened takes it seriously, then you should, too, even if the perpetrator says it was a joke)
- makes even joking threats repeatedly or in writing
- plays pranks or practical jokes that actually endanger people
- is discovered to have a habit of violence or abuse
- commits a violent crime

In such cases, Human Resources should be involved and the employee should, at a minimum, be asked to enroll in an anger management program and be placed in some type of probationary status.

Legally, these situations can become quite complex, as the company has responsibilities, both to the employee engaging in the behavior and also to other employees. Be sure to do the following:

- Take the situation seriously and document it in writing.
- Take a look at Chapter 20, When to Get Help.
- Get expert advice.

- Keep confidentiality where appropriate.
- Build the team and support good communication.
- Pay close attention both to the person performing the troubling actions and to those who receive the brunt of it.
- Once you have gotten expert advice, take firm, clear action and stick to your decisions.
- Be open to the possibility of growth and change, but require very clear proof that the work environment will remain healthy and safe for everyone.

Even if we are attentive to all of the signs, there is always the lingering fear that comes from news stories about the employee who seemed completely harmless until he came in and shot up the office. Yes, these things do happen— quite rarely. And no, we should not allow them to scare us. Prevention is the best medicine. And a team that works together, communicates well, makes room for friendships, and builds trust is the best prevention.

"Why Are You Always Angry at Me?"

Sometimes, an employee develops an ongoing attitude of anger or defensiveness toward you as his manager. This prevents effective communication and coaching and creates a situation that makes it difficult for the team member to grow and improve. A person who is angry or defensive is closed to learning.

We may want to ask, "Why are you always angry or defensive with me?" but it is probably better to phrase it *"It seems that something is getting in the way here, and you're not working with what I have to say."* The biggest difficulty in these kinds of situations is that, for a good solution, we must break through the angry, defensive lack of listening on the other side. We can ask for this, but only the team member can make it happen.

We need to be gentle, but clear. *I want to improve our working relationship and I want you to help me* sets the right tone. We need to be steady and persistent. Sometimes, if the team member refuses to acknowledge or deal with the problem, we may need to be insistent, as well. But we must be gentle, because underneath the defensiveness and anger is probably some hurt feeling that may come from a prior interaction with us, a misunderstanding of our tone or intention, or a memory of some other work situation or other experience.

"You Sure Sound Angry to Me"

Some people sound angry to others even when they are not angry. The person may just feel frustrated, or simply urgent, or even misunderstood. But others interpret that as anger or criticism.

In this case, we need to let the person know: *Whether you are angry or not, you sound angry to others.* If the team member says he is not angry, then say, *"You are responsible for how you seem to others, for the impression you give. Please find some different choice of words or different tone, so that people will know how you really feel. Then, they'll be more responsive."*

Most people want to be understood and will work with this idea. If a team member says something like *"I don't care what others think,"* then something deeper is at work. Say, *"Many of us do care. We want a harmonious team. Will you help?"* Then listen, and perhaps the team member will identify a deeper concern you can work with.

The Team Is About to Explode

Sometimes, the entire team gets tense or angry. There may be a specific trigger, such as the cancellation of a project, the cutting of a budget, or an unreasonable deadline. Or the problem may be chronic—such as underfunding or under-appreciation.

Telling the team members what is wrong won't help, even if you know. To discharge their feelings, they have to say it themselves. Bring everyone together and ask, *"OK, what's bugging you?"* If you have to, say, *"I won't leave until we talk about it."* If someone says, "You know what's bugging us," then say, *"Yes, but I want each of you to say how it feels to you. That's the first step."* This is important, because, even when we're all angry about the same thing, we all feel it a bit differently.

Once the team voices its feelings, you can find an appropriate response. It may be something like this: *"The company doesn't appreciate us and doesn't give us enough resources to do our job. But we appreciate one another and stick together."* Then find some way to bring in a bit of fun or humor. After that, express your appreciation for each member of the team. Then, sit down and work out a new battle plan. Why do I call it a battle plan? Because the team is working under siege. Make sure the team understands that the battle is to do good work in a difficult situation, not to fight the company.

Now I'm the One Who's Angry

What do we do when we get angry? It's natural to get angry sometimes, but it puts us in a challenging position for three reasons:

- We've asked the team to handle their anger well. We must be an exceptional model to keep our integrity, to walk our own talk.
- We are in a position of authority. Anger from us is much more threatening than it is from an equal, and fear of that anger can reduce performance for a long time.
- We are part of the team, but different. Our anger can pull the team away from us or even set it against us.

The most important step we can take is to separate our anger from the issue. There are many techniques to help with this. Three I like are:

- Slow down and breathe.
- Take a walk.
- Write down your feelings and thoughts about the issue in a business journal. Note: It's a good idea to delete this entry after you take care of the issue.

Once the anger and the issue are separate, I am ready to work with the team. If I expressed anger or even frustration, I open with an apology. Then I explain that I took time to separate my anger from the issue. I then present the issue either as a gap to be closed or as my perception of a situation that needs to be changed. From there, I actively engage my team in a positive way to resolve the problem.

What If the Top Boss Is Angry?

Sometimes, we work in a company where anger comes down from the top and shapes the whole organization. (Some might say that this happens all too often in American business.) In such a situation, we, as managers, become shock absorbers. As best we can, we take the anger from above and try to protect our team. But we will need a way to release that excess pressure. And, when the pressure hits the team, it will bend the whole team out of shape. Then, we need to find a way to straighten everything out.

Appreciation, humor, and recognition of the situation are good medicine. So is reframing: *We work for the company, not the boss. We're here to do good work, serve the customer, and make a living for ourselves.* Ideas like this show the situation from a new angle, giving the boss less power in the mind of the team. *The boss is just one player, not the whole team.*

Chapter 14
Fear in the Office

Fear—whether realistic or not—is a performance killer. Managing a fearful employee requires understanding the basis of the fear and helping him face the real situation with confidence. When there's fear, there's no room for improvement. The fear takes up all the space.

People handle fear differently. For some of us, we accept fear and uncertainty on the job as just they way things are and keep working toward our goal. For others, fear is paralyzing. Psychologists classify our responses to fear and anger into personality types, but we don't need to be psychologists to be good managers. We do need to understand that people respond differently to criticism. Something you say may be a reasonable course correction for one person and induce paralyzing fear in someone else on the same team. We need to learn to gauge how to provide direction and guidance to each person on our team.

Some people are afraid of talking about fear. So, it can be useful to use gentler words, such as *upset*, *anxious*, or *worried*.

W. Edwards Deming, the founder of the quality management movement, defined the elimination of fear as one of the key guiding principles for any company that wants to promote excellence and continuously improving performance. He was right: fear is a barrier to productivity and success. We can't always eliminate fear; when we can't, we should do our best to manage it.

Fear of Bringing Up Problems

Some team members are unaware of their fear, and we notice it before they do. They become less responsive, either verbally or in delivering their work. Often, when we ask what the problem is, they say, "Nothing."

In this situation, we need to confront the problem without confronting the person—and he probably doesn't know the difference.

Here is one way to handle the situation. Come up with a specific piece of evidence—an instruction not followed, a piece of work not delivered. Sit down with the team member and say, "*I know something's gone wrong recently. You usually do just fine on this kind of work, but this time, this happened. [Show the problem.] I'm wondering if there is something in the system causing this problem or just what is causing it, so we can work together to fix it.*

For others, a more direct approach can work: *I know there's something making you uncomfortable, and it's hard to talk about. But, to keep the work moving, we need to clear the air. Did I do something wrong?* That last question, *Did I do something wrong?* will often bring out fellow-feeling from someone who is feeling insecure, nervous, or scared.

Employees Who Fear Making a Mistake

Mistakes are a part of business because they are a part of life. But some people grew up or worked in environments where mistakes were disastrous. What can we do if a team member refuses an assignment or avoids a situation, saying, "I'm afraid of making a mistake"?

Walk him through the work: *Let's see what would happen if you made a mistake.* Go through whatever the work is, step by step. Have the team member pick a mistake he might make. Show what would happen. Show how he would handle it, with help from you or the team. And, finally, show him what he would learn from the mistake.

Then tell a story of your own where you took on a job, made a mistake, and learned from it. Say, *"Making mistakes, correcting them, and learning from them is part of our work here. As long as there are people, there will be mistakes. We need to be willing to make mistakes, because it's the same as being willing to work, learn, and grow."*

Employees Who Fear the Manager

Sometimes, we discover that a team member is afraid of us—and it surprises us. Looking back from our own perspective, we don't think we got angry, we can't recall doing anything hurtful. One of two things has happened: either we don't know ourselves as well as we thought we did or the team member is misinterpreting or overreacting, possibly because of the power we hold.

With some people, it might work to say, *"You're afraid of me?"* with genuine surprise. But it is probably better to open with an apology. *I'm not sure what I did to scare you, but I certainly didn't mean to. Please tell me how it looked from your side.* When you hear how it sounded, you will probably be able to say something that falls into one of these two categories:

- *I'm sorry I gave that impression. That wasn't what I meant at all.* You might go on to explain that you were actually upset about something else that day or that you could have chosen your words more carefully.
- *I'm sorry, I was a bit frustrated, not angry, and certainly not at you.* This works if the team member overreacted.

In either case, move the conversation toward ways of understanding each other better in the future. Tell the team member what you've learned about working with him and ask him to tell you what he's learned about listening to you. You might end with *If I make you nervous again, let me know, and we'll work it out* or *If you think I'm angry at you, just ask.* Your goal is to create a working relationship where communication is not blocked or slowed down too much by fear.

Fear of Being Laid Off

If an employee is on probation, close to a layoff, or in any situation where his job might end, fear is nearly inevitable. However, even if the final decision—such as termination—is up to us, we should do our best to stay on the same side with the team member right up through the end. There are two reasons. The cost of hiring, training, and orienting new people is high. Also, the credibility we gain with our team and with management by helping a poor performer become a good team player makes the effort worthwhile.

On the principle of starting from where we are, with honesty, say, *"You might lose your job, but I want to help."* You can continue by saying something like *I want to make it as clear as I can what you need to do and what results you need to achieve. Then you'll need to let me know if you have everything you need or if there is anything else I can do.* You might end with *Let's put the past behind us and make this work.*

Fear from Outside the Office

Even if we can create a healthy work environment with little or no fear, fear will enter the workplace from outside. Here are some common sources of fear from outside the office:

- Someone from outside the office—perhaps a team member's spouse or partner—comes to the office and makes a scene.
- Employees have a frightening situation in their home life—children going to a dangerous school, an elderly or sick relative in the hospital—and come to work distracted and afraid.
- People may need to travel through dangerous or uncomfortable situations—highways with narrow lanes, busses, or walks through bad neighborhoods—to get to work.
- General social conditions, such as war and economic instability, are sources of fear.
- Catastrophic news shocks everyone. We all experienced this when we heard about the attacks on 9/11.

People master their fear by learning to breathe, relax, and focus. The key is *Fear gets in the way of work, but work also gets in the way of fear.* When we can relax and focus on work, we lessen the physiological effects of fear, which can be distracting or even paralyzing. If we focus closely on our work and appreciate each small success, we can find joy, even in times of difficulty.

Employees with Depression or Anxiety

For some people, fear is a deeper part of their personality or life situation. This includes psychological conditions—especially depression and anxiety—and abusive or unsafe situations at home or in relationships. It can be difficult to accept that these things are a part of the lives of the people we work with, but all too often they are.

We all go through ups and downs, and it can be difficult to distinguish between normal mood fluctuations and a truly dangerous condition or situation. Here are some things to keep an eye on:

- Chronic inability to complete a full work day or full work week
- Extreme fluctuations in attendance or productivity
- Greater reticence than usual in talking about what is going on
- Disconnection from work and lack of motivation

If you see these kinds of problems and simple overtures of support aren't effective, see Chapter 20, When to Get Help.

EXAMPLE: FEAR IN THE WORST SITUATION

Some people could think that what I've written here is unrealistic. The truth is, some people have mastered fear even in situations far more difficult than yours. For example, read Victor Frankl's *Man's Search for Meaning*. Frankl survived the Auschwitz concentration camp during World War II and helped hundreds of others survive as well. Then he went on to create Logotherapy, an approach to growth and healing based on defining meaning in our lives.

Chapter 15
Illness Issues

Employee illness is a reason for compassion. It also generates concern about productivity and other office issues. Misuse of sick leave can also be a problem. As managers, we also have to be aware of company rules and legal requirements regarding employee disability, pregnancy, and unpaid leaves of absence.

Is the Employee Really Sick?

Sometimes, something makes us wonder whether a team member's stories of illness are true. It may be a pattern of behavior, such as arriving late with claims of illness after party nights, or an illness without clear symptoms. In these circumstances, we probably don't want to break into the team member's personal life by asking, "Are you really sick?"

Instead, discuss these points:

- How many sick days the employee has left
- The correct way to give notice when using personal leave for illness or when going to a scheduled doctor's appointment
- The effects of the absence on productivity and project goals

Ask the employee if he wants to talk about anything else, but don't probe. Caution the employee that, if he uses up all his personal days, it will be necessary for his doctor to write a letter explaining when he needs to be away from work and when he can return. Say that the letter does not need to include the diagnosis—the name of the illness.

If the employee wants to explain the illness or to discuss other options, such as working from home, you can have the discussion. But also be sure to include a consultation with HR or a human resources consultant, because awareness of an employee's illness changes your rights and responsibilities under the Family and Medical Leave Act (FMLA) and the Americans with Disabilities Act (ADA).

Friday Flu

Sometimes, the pattern of a person's sick days indicates that illness isn't really the issue. A regular Friday or Monday illness can be a way to get a long weekend. Any other recurring schedule that is called sick time but not scheduled in advance, the way a doctor's visit would be, is an indicator that something else may be going on.

When an employee does this, it affects work in two ways. First, unscheduled absence is a strain on the team: someone will have to shift things around to get the work done or to work around what didn't get done. Second, when a team member develops a habit of not being clear and truthful, it reduces our ability to work together as a team.

While the team member might just be getting out of town for long weekends, we can't assume that is the case. The person might have a legitimate reason for taking the time and stretching the truth. Open with *"I've noticed a pattern in your personal leave days and I'd like to talk about it."* Be gentle, even if you're headed for a confrontation, because you want to give the person a chance to make things right.

Here are two examples of what might be happening and how you can handle them:

- The person has a medical condition that requires regular, scheduled treatment, but doesn't want you to know the appointment in advance, because then you would know that there is a condition, not just occasional illness. You can say, *"I want to work with you, but the team needs help, too. We can't handle your absence this frequently without notice—when we could have notice. Let me know the schedule, and we'll give you the time off. We can say nothing or we can say that you're going for some tests. But no one here—not even me—has any reason to know what your diagnosis is."*

- The person is overcome by work stress, whether due to anxiety, mobbing, or some other cause. He is coping by avoiding Mondays or leaving on Fridays or being sick to miss the weekly staff meeting. If this comes up, you can say, *"We need to solve this problem, not just put a bandage on it. Let's get rid of the source of the stress and help you feel better working here."*

What do you do if the employee admits to running off on Friday to go play in her new speedboat? Smile and say, *"Now that you've been busted, let's go over the ground rules."* Explain that it is not fair to the team to take unannounced leave for vacation purposes. Advanced notice and approval are necessary. Then decide what is a fair and workable flex schedule—if there is one—to make room for the new hobby. Your solution has to be in accordance with company policy and be fair to everyone on the team. But maybe a good flex alternative can be worked out for everyone on the team, reducing stress while increasing loyalty and productivity.

Showing Up Sick at Work

When someone shows up sick at work or gets sick during the day, the best thing is to send him home. And that applies to us, as well: we set a better example for the team by leading a balanced life than by being a workaholic hero. However, there are some things we need to consider:

- Is it safe for the person to go travel? If he is dizzy or blacking out or very weak, driving or using public transportation may not be safe.
- Will the person be safe at home? Will someone be there with him? If there is no one at home, it might not be best for him to be sick at home.
- Might the illness be contagious?

We want to take care of a sick team member, but, unfortunately, we need to be careful about the boundary between work life and personal life. There was an incident where a boss decided it wasn't good for an employee to take the bus home, so he had the office pay for a taxi to take the person home. Something went wrong on the taxi ride, and—as strange as it may seem—because the company had paid for the ride, the company was held liable. You might want to talk with your HR department or an HR consultant to find out what options you have to help employees who get sick at work.

Frequent but Unpredictable Illness

What do you do if someone is taking sick time often, but not on a predictable schedule? This could be a sign of any of several things:

- The person is just having a run of bad luck with his health.
- The person has a health issue that is more serious than he realizes or has been misdiagnosed. For example, what looks like a cold or the flu might have developed into pneumonia or might be serious allergies.
- The person is having problems with drugs or alcohol.

Open a conversation by saying, *"I've noticed that you've been out sick lately and I'm concerned."* Make it clear that you don't want to know the diagnosis—you only want to make sure that he is getting good diagnosis and good treatment. As long as you think the employee is being honest and taking good care of himself, so much the better. If you think the person is honest but, like many of us, tends to minimize illness or avoid doctors, then say, *"You're a key player on this team; we miss your contribution when you're sick. Would you get a checkup to take care of the team?"* People who won't go to doctors—or wear seatbelts or do anything to take care of their health and safety—for themselves will often do it when shown how it helps others.

What do you do if you think the employee is not being fully honest and cooperative, possibly due to a substance abuse problem? First of all, if your company offers an employee assistance program (EAP), you should encourage him to go. If you don't want to raise the issue of substance abuse, you can say, *"I know how stressful it can be to be sick this much. You might use the EAP to help with the stress or any other problems you are having."* You can also say, *"With this many absences, I need a letter from your doctor. It doesn't need to give a diagnosis. I just need the letter, signed by your doctor, saying that you are under treatment and letting me know of any treatment schedule and any limitations this might pose on your ability to work."* If the employee says that he is seeing a doctor, but doesn't bring in this letter promptly, then that can be a sign that the employee is hiding something.

If you want to somehow open the door to the issue of substance abuse without confronting the employee, then you can review the company drug policy with the entire team. Don't single anyone out unless you are sure. Drug abuse at work raises complicated legal issues because of the conflict between an employee's right to privacy and a company's right to know. See Chapter 20, When to Get Help, for more information.

"I Think There's Something Wrong with Him"

What do we do when one employee comes to us with a medical concern or a concern regarding substance abuse, addiction, or psychological problems about another team member?

The key is confidentiality. Get a list of observable facts or symptoms from the person raising the issue. Then tell him that, in order to protect both his privacy and the privacy of the team member who might have a problem, you need to handle this confidentially and he should say nothing more about it to anyone.

At that point, you should consult HR or contact an HR consultant. With that guidance, it may be appropriate to meet with the employee. Open with *"Some things have come to my attention. This meeting is completely confidential and you don't have to explain anything personal to me."* Then lay out factual, practical concerns about work and things seen at work. Let the employee know about the company's employee assistance program or any other resources that might be available. Ask for assurance that the employee is taking good care of himself and seeking appropriate professional assistance. If appropriate, you can request a doctor's letter, as described in the previous situation.

Illnesses in the Family

Our team members will sometimes have to handle an urgent health problem in the family, such as a child sick at school or a parent with sudden illness.

If these events are occasional, then family life is more important than work at these moments. We and other members of the team should do what is necessary to help resolve the situation so everyone is well taken care of.

However, if an employee has a chronically ill child, parent, or partner, then you want to work out an agreement that will take care of the situation for the team and the company, as well as for the person and his family. Make a list of your work concerns—such as important goals for routine work and for projects and the need for the team member to keep the team informed—and also what you can offer in terms of flexible work hours, leave, an employee assistance program to help with stress, or other resources.

The employee may want to avoid the issue by saying that it will be resolved soon. If so, say, *"I hope it will be. But, when it comes to illness, none of us can be sure. Let's plan for the long term, so we can handle it if we have to."*

Note that we and the company are best off if we treat everyone's family—whether it is a traditional family or a same-sex partnership—just the same. When team members know that the team, the boss, and the company care about a balance of family life and work, then they care about the work, the team, and the company and are more loyal.

Illness Interfering with Business Travel

If a team member travels as part of his job, then the combination of illness and travel make can make things difficult and complicated. Being sick on the road is a miserable experience—I've been there—and it takes longer to recover when we are ill away from home. If travel is international or to remote areas, there can also be concerns about the quality of available medical care.

Prevention is the first step. Strongly encourage team members who travel to take up exercise and keep a healthy diet. *Travel demands a lot and wears us out.*

If someone gets sick before a trip, cancel it or send someone in his place. It doesn't make sense to pressure someone to travel and work when he is ill—the risks are too high.

If someone gets sick on the road, his care is the most important thing. Make sure he is treated by a doctor or in a clinic. Let a doctor decide if he is fit to work and if he is better off recovering in a hotel away from home or in a hospital or traveling home. For example, it might be better for people with ear and sinus infections to recover before they fly, due to the change in air pressure and its effect on sinuses.

If a team member develops a chronic condition that inhibits travel and travel is part of the job, then sit down with the team member to clarify the options. Can the job be adjusted to include less travel or a type of travel that is less stressful? Is there a position open that does not require travel? In short, put the team member first and the work second.

Pregnancy and Illness

Pregnancy is not an illness. It is a medical condition and, in some cases, complications or illnesses can arise during pregnancy. In addition, pregnancy is a condition that calls for avoiding exposure to alcohol and environmental toxins. In the later months, there should be restrictions on lifting and physical activity. If you learn a team member is pregnant, ask your HR department for guidance. If you are in a company without an HR department, ask for a letter from or a consultation with the team member's obstetrician to discuss what changes in work routine—if any—are appropriate.

Requests for Unpaid Leave or Disability

When an employee's need for leave exceeds his available total personal leave time, the company faces a choice—a choice restricted by the Americans with Disabilities Act (ADA) in some cases.

It is essential to keep on top of your team member's available personal leave time. If he is close to using it up, familiarize yourself with policies for unpaid leave or turn the issue over to HR. If you work for a small company without an HR department, you should retain a consultant who can guide you in developing a legally acceptable policy.

Be aware that one thing that makes sense for a business is not an acceptable or safe practice. It might seem to make sense to extend more leave for a more effective employee; after all, this is a person who would be more valuable to retain. However, any time we treat different employees differently, we open up the company to charges of discrimination. So, make a policy—and then apply it fairly.

Chapter 16
Failure—Employee
or Company

Sometimes, a project falls through, a team member's work is so poor that we need to let him go, or the company has to make layoffs. A manager's approach in these difficult situations is the difference between the office pulling together and the office falling apart.

Employee on the Edge

Initially, we always take an optimistic approach, believing that, with coaching, our team members can resolve difficult situations and stay with us. There is good reason for this: study after study shows that employees rarely exceed their boss's expectations. So, it pays to expect the best.

Our optimism must not cloud our realism. If it does, we are not serving the company or the team or the team member with the problem. Excessive, unrealistic loyalty and hope only serve to increase cost, increase damage, throw the team off balance, and leave everyone worse off in the end.

For this reason, each solution requires a clear goal—a deliverable or a demonstrated change of habit—and a due date. I call it a due date, not a deadline, because no one is dying. It doesn't help to introduce fear. But it does help to be clear about consequences.

In resolving difficult situations, we may need to go a little further. If a team member doesn't follow the first plan and meet the first goal, we don't throw him out the door. How many more chances does he get? That depends. We need to consider the criticality of the problem, its cost, HR and union rules governing warnings and termination, the amount of progress, and—above all—the team member's honest willingness to solve the problem.

Some companies have clear rules regarding reasons for immediate termination. Usually, these have to do either with safety or with serious ethical violations. If the company ensures that every employee knows the rules, then it is correct to terminate someone on first violation of those rules. Be sure you know the policies and their consequences. For example, construction companies often have a zero-tolerance policy for drug abuse (unless the employee steps forward and asks for help first) and publishers may have a zero tolerance policy for plagiarism.

Our main concern, though, is the gray areas where we have to evaluate performance and progress and decide if an employee is solving the problem soon enough to make things work. As we come to this evaluation, we should get clear on these questions:

- *How many chances has the team member had already?* We should avoid vague extended deadlines or changes of the goal. Each time, the team member either succeeds or fails, and the next step is laid out clearly.
- *How big is the gap?* How big was the problem to begin with? How much progress has been made?
- *Is the team member getting sufficient guidance, support, and resources?* At each meeting, make sure the team member agrees that he understands what to do and how to do it and has everything he needs.
- *How big is the change?* This cuts both ways. If the change is small, then why hasn't the team member succeeded already? There may be deeper problems. If the change is large, then the employee may not be able to make it.
- *Is the team member on board, honestly willing to put his best effort into making the change?* If the team member is not clear about the problem, honest with us, and sin-

cere in his efforts, chances of success are small.

- *What are the costs?* We have to look at both sides: What are the costs of giving the employee another chance and having him fail? What are the costs of letting go of the employee? And we need to look at soft costs—costs that are hard to measure, such as team morale—as well as the bottom line in dollars.

It is difficult to move toward letting go of an employee. We don't want to fire people, to disrupt their lives and their self-esteem. We may not want to face admitting a hiring mistake or the work of hiring a replacement. That is why the last point—the evaluation of cost—is so important. We need to remember our responsibility to our company and balance it against our support of the team member who is having trouble and the cost of hiring a replacement.

When we are clear on these points, we are ready to set up a final opportunity for the team member to solve the problem. As before, we set a clear goal and a target date. We coordinate our efforts with HR, to make sure we are complying with all rules related to warnings and termination. Then we add, *"I still hope you can do this, and I'll support you all I can. But you need to know: this is your last chance to make things work. If we clearly have these results by this date, you can keep your job. Otherwise, I'll have to let you go."* Then set up appropriate interim dates to track progress and provide support.

"I've Got to Let You Go"

If we've done all the steps in the previous situation and the employee still has not resolved the problem, it is time to take the difficult step of firing the employee. I've been fired and I've let people go. It is not easy. But I have found one consistent fact in all of my experience: if we've done the best we can and followed these steps clearly, it is for the best. Clearly, it is best for the company—and, in my experience, it is best for the employee. Business situations that don't work out are usually bad matches; the person doesn't match the job or the team. When a team member leaves—even if forced to leave—he or she can go on to find a better match. I've done that and I've helped employees who I've let go do that, as well. No matter how badly things turn out, I wish people well. Whether the next step is a new job, retirement, or a drug rehabilitation program, may they go into it well, learn, and succeed.

Prepare yourself emotionally and also get all the facts clear. What is the employee's last day? Is there a severance package? Is this a layoff, so that the employee is entitled to unemployment benefits? Or is it termination with cause, in which case you are saying the employee is not entitled? What are the employee's options for continuing medical coverage?

It may be up to you to decide whether the team member leaves immediately or stays to wrap things up. Here are the things you should consider:

- Two weeks' notice is a good idea—if it will work. In

my experience, two weeks is a good amount of time for a team member to wrap up work and say goodbye. Longer that that seems to create discomfort for everyone and waste time. But read on for reasons to end before two weeks is out.

- If the issues are related to dishonesty, criminal activity, or substance abuse, immediate departure is probably best. Plan on giving two weeks' severance pay. Also, if appropriate, provide some supervised time where the team member is in meetings to explain the status of work and transfer any unfinished jobs.

- If the employee has access to secure or proprietary information, responsibility for security, or administrative control of the computer system, departure should be immediate. This is necessary for two reasons. First of all, it reduces the possibility of sabotage. Second, if anything goes wrong later and the departing employee had a chance to make it happen, there will be a cloud of suspicion, which is unfair if the employee is innocent.

When the plan is ready and the facts are clear, stop and breathe to take care of yourself. Meet with the employee and review the last agreement you had for what he needed to do. Then say, *"I'm sorry, but we haven't been able to solve this problem. I'm going to have to let you go."* Make sure the employee really takes this in and understands it. Then, take time to listen. Often, the employee will feel acceptance or have a sense of what to do next. Simply be a good listener—you've already learned you are not the right coach for this person. Go over the steps and procedures of termination, making sure everything is clear. As a last step, deliver a letter of termination and have him sign a copy.

EXAMPLE: THANKS FOR LAYING ME OFF

One time, I spent eight months in a job that wasn't well suited for me. I wasn't too long out of college, and I was a tax assistant for a CPA firm. The stress of keeping track of over a thousand tax returns for three months wasn't good for me. I did a good job and survived tax season. But I had decided to leave and started to look for new work.

The four partners of the firm held an unusual meeting and they were calling in each employee, one by one. Each person left grim-faced and silent. Whatever was going on—and we really didn't know—it wasn't good.

My turn came. The partners explained that two of them had decided that the commute into Manhattan was too difficult and that the office was being split up. There would be a small office in New York and a new one in New Jersey. And most employees were being laid off, including me.

I said, "This must be a really difficult day for you. For me, though, this is the best thing that could have happened. I had already decided that I didn't fit in, and I didn't know how to tell you I would be leaving. Now, because of your decision, I will stay until the end of my job, help all I can, and collect unemployment unless I find a new job first."

I stood up, shook each one's hand, thanked them for laying me off, and made their day a little brighter.

The lesson: whatever happens at work, life goes on. When we have to let go, it is often better for everyone.

When Projects Fail

When a team or a team member is focused on an important project, it can seem like it's the whole world. We encourage ourselves by saying, "This marketing campaign will give us the money to stay in business" or "This new computer program will solve our inventory problems." Then we run the marketing campaign, but no one buys, or the new computer system never even works.

Reframing is the key: *"The project is over and we're still here."* Then take time to listen. Let people vent, but realize that it is probably too soon for a project review of any real value. That can come later. Listen to people as they let go of the old project. Then ask, *"Where are we today? What matters now?"*

Start a fresh brainstorming session about the status and needs of the department. Listen and also contribute your own ideas. Sometimes, there is a need to focus on catching up on routine work that has fallen behind. Other times, a new project or area of focus is most urgent. Before we try to fix the mess left by the failed project, we should make sure we are taking care of everything else.

Think of it this way: *First, focus on the team and rebuild the team. Then, start new work.*

"We're Waiting to Hear"

Sometimes, the whole team is left waiting in anxious anticipation. We might be waiting to hear from management. Is the whole project cancelled? Is the whole team being laid off? Or we might be waiting to hear from customers. Is our new marketing campaign working? Did we get the big contract? Everyone knows it matters, but there's nothing we can do about it.

How do we hold a team together in a time like this? We have two choices:

- *Let's focus on something else.* Maybe this is a good time to catch up on back work, to clear the stack of problems we thought we'd never get around to, to look at other areas of responsibility or alternatives. This option is especially good when the decision is not about the end of the team. For example, if we're waiting to hear about a huge contract, we can say, "Let's figure we're not going to get it. What can we do to be ready? Are we up to date on work for other clients? What are our other hot leads, even if they're small?" Doing this work keeps people busy and focused, and it's useful, either way, whether we get the contract or not.
- *Let's chill.* If the fate of the whole team—or a large piece of it—is on the line, this may be the best option. There are many ways of doing this. You can just be OK with the fact that the people on our team are sitting at their desks doing nothing. Or you can tell everyone to go home early. Or you can declare a pizza party. *For now, the team has no goal. So, take care of the team.*

Early Retirement Issues

Larger companies and government agencies often find value in offering early retirement plans. There are at least two reasons for this:

- If the company needs to downsize, reduce its total staff, encouraging early voluntary departure is less costly and damaging than deciding who to lay off.
- Employees with longer tenure cost more. It can be less expensive to pay them to leave early and then fill the slots with younger, less experienced people at a lower starting salary.

Be clear about the company's goals for the plan and your own feelings about it. Then, manage the implementation of the plan in the way that best suits your department. You must inform everyone of the plan and help each person understand how it applies to him or her. This can be very complicated, so make sure each employee reviews his options with HR. Also encourage team members to discuss the package with their families and decide what is best.

Once this is done, you can choose whom you encourage to stay and whom you encourage to accept the retirement package. But do it gently. If someone decides to stay, you don't want to leave him thinking, "The boss wanted to get rid of me, but I stayed." That's a sure recipe for a difficult and unproductive relationship.

Ask the entire team to work together to update job descriptions, write standard operating procedures (SOPs), and cross-train. You may want to set up a system called "ghosting," where each employee learns another team member's job as a backup. This is a good general management approach, as it provides coverage for vacations and any other situation where a team member isn't working. If you are doing it in preparation for early retirement and a reorganization, make sure that the "ghosts"—the people learning other jobs—are ones who have said they will stay or, at least, are likely to stay.

"The Company's Laying You Off"

It's difficult to present a layoff to one of our team members. Sometimes, we have to choose who gets laid off. Other times, company rules—such as seniority—or company plans—such as cancellation of a project, product line, or service—govern the choice. Either way, it is not easy.

First, get all the information that you can for the employee. Plan the termination date, the severance package, and all the other details. Find out who the employee should talk with in HR and if the company offers placement assistance. Find out what options are available for applying for other positions in the firm and what the policy is regarding recall of employees who are being laid off. Also, find out where the employee should go to apply for unemployment benefits.

If you work for a reasonably well-run company and you've been keeping your team informed, then the layoff should not come as a total surprise. Still, even when expected, layoffs are a shock.

Be simple and straightforward: *"I'm sorry, but the company is laying you off."* Then listen. Walk the employee through the steps and the materials you've offered and then help him follow through. End with *"Is there anything I can do to help?"* Follow up with the employee through his final day to make sure he is doing at least something to adjust to the situation.

"The Company's Laying Us Off"

In the last job I had before I started my own company, I was a computer manager for a graduate school. After I'd been there six months, I remember thinking on the way to work: I've been here six months, the dean (my boss) loves me, all the professors really appreciate me, the computer lab is running well, and the students think it's great. What could go wrong?

That day, the university announced that it was closing the entire graduate school and throwing us all out in the street.

What do we say when we're being laid off, along with some or all of our team? First, we prepare in the same way as we would for the individual layoffs we described in the previous situation. Then we bring the team together to let them know. *"The company has decided to lay all of us (or some of us) off."* If it's not everyone, make sure that each person understands his or her own situation. Then go on to say something like this: *"Although we won't be a team any more, I hope that what we've been doing will continue in each of your lives. You're all professionals, and you've become better professionals and team players while you were here. I encourage you to continue to grow in your careers and to make a clear and positive choice of where you want to go next. When you get there, be sure to build a good team. Keep moving toward your own goals."* Then, take time to describe what you are going to do— name just one or two positive steps. And, for the rest of your time, do what you can to support each team member in finding a good situation.

Chapter 17
Emergencies

njuries at work, news of national disasters like 9/11, and other dangerous situations call on us to make sure everyone is safe, get care for those who need help, give out appropriate information to protect privacy and reduce the spread of rumors, and help the team focus appropriately. And we have to do it all at once.

EXAMPLE: EMERGENCY PREPAREDNESS

Having an emergency evacuation plan isn't enough. There's a wonderful episode of the TV show *ER* where they have to evacuate the emergency room—and no one can find the evacuation plan. Planning for emergencies requires contingencies—such as what to do if an exit is blocked or if power goes out—and rehearsals and assignment of responsibilities.

Major Illness in the Office

How prepared is your office for a medical emergency? Does anyone know CPR and first aid for shock, bleeding, and injuries? If so, do you know who that is? How often is he or she in the office? Do you know where the first aid kit is?

When an emergency happens, the first and most important thing is to provide care to the ill or injured person. Immediately do four things:

- Have someone stay with the patient.
- Call for whoever in the office knows first aid.
- Call 911 and follow their instructions.
- Have someone—not the person making the call to 911 or the person taking care of the patient—direct people out of the way, doing crowd control or managing traffic. *"Please go back to work for now, and we'll let you know what happened as soon as we can."* If necessary, add, *"We need to make room for the emergency medical technicians."*

Once the patient is receiving proper care, we can turn our attention to our team. Be aware of these issues:

- *Early on, we may not know the whole story.* People always want to know everything, right away, but that just isn't possible. We won't know the whole story until the doctors do, which is after emergency treatment, diagnosis, and initial care. Help people understand that it may be hours or days before a clear report is available.
- *Privacy is at risk.* Even an innocent question such as "What happened?" can be difficult to answer. For

example, if you know—confidentially—that a team member has a chronic illness that is related to the emergency, then explaining the emergency could reveal too much about the confidential medical condition. *Privacy is more important than curiosity—or even genuine concern.*

- *"We're still at the office"* is a reminder that will help people return to work and wait until a meaningful update is available. *"I'll keep on top of this and keep everyone posted"* is useful for reassurance.

Afterwards, do keep on top of it and keep everyone posted or assign a team member to do so. When you do, explain to the patient, *"People saw the ambulance come and they're all concerned for you. But you don't have to tell them anything you don't want to. We can just tell them that you're doing OK and when you might be back. Or, do you have something you want me to pass along?"* If the person is going to have an extended leave or hospital stay, the team should get together and give one card or gift, to keep things simple. Of course, any friend of the patient is welcome to do more, as well.

"Is Everyone OK?"

Emergencies can be confusing. If everyone evacuates in an office fire, are you sure everyone got out? Are you sure that everyone is OK—not only not caught in the fire, but that no one fell downstairs or got exhausted climbing down 15 floors to the lobby? Try to find everyone and, as you find each person, ask him to stay in one place. Then have one or two people look around for others.

Ideally, you should have an evacuation plan and conduct periodic fire drills. If you do, there may be someone appointed as a fire marshal to make sure everyone leaves, take care of security, and leave last. If not, then consider this your job. *The safety of other people is first, your safety is second, and the safety of confidential information and other property is third.*

Try to bring everyone together before they wander off. As you see each person, say, *"Stay together at [location], but, if someone does have to leave, make sure that they tell you where they're going, so we can know everyone is OK."*

Once everyone is together, decide what to do. Ask people if they left behind personal possessions—especially essentials such as car keys or very valuable items. Make a list of those items, and do what you need to take care of people. If it is near the end of the day and it may be a while before anyone can get into the building, it may be best to declare the rest of the day off. Also pay attention to whether one person—perhaps you—should stay nearby to secure the office once people can get back in.

Disaster Strikes

When the space shuttle Challenger exploded on takeoff, I was working for a small company and the UPS driver brought the news. The boss pulled out a portable TV—I didn't even know we had one—and we watched what was happening. When disaster strikes or war is declared or peace is declared, our roles as people in society and as citizens are more important than our jobs with the company. And having the team members together to support one another is healthy for everyone and for the team.

At the same time, we need to be cautious about obsession and distraction. If there is no new news and the TV newscasters are endlessly recycling video footage or old reports, it might be best to encourage everyone to get back to work. Assign one person to listen to the radio or check the TV every 15 minutes. Then help people refocus. At the same time, be aware of anyone with special needs. For example, if war is declared and a team member has a child in the armed forces overseas, it is reasonable to let that person have off until the end of the day if he wants it.

What Happened to Him?

After an injury or illness in the office, people want to know what happened. We should manage the flow of information. We can prevent rumors by providing clear information—even if it is minimal—periodically at appropriate times. For example, if a team member is on leave or has an extended hospital stay, then it is a good idea to update everyone on his condition at the weekly staff meeting or to post a note on the office bulletin board saying how he is doing and whether he would like calls or visitors.

Take responsibility to manage information and keep everyone posted. That's a lot easier than trying to quash rumors later. It also protects people's privacy and confidential information, because you control what information is being sent out.

"We Just Don't Know What's Happening"

In some situations, we just don't know what is happening. For example, if the team works in a large office tower, we might have to evacuate due to a fire alarm without ever knowing where the fire was—or if it was a false alarm. Or, if a team member had a heart attack or a stroke, it may be weeks before we know how well he is doing and if he will be able to return to work.

It is still important to keep people posted. Saying, *"We don't know anything new"* is much better than not saying anything at all. And keep track of your bulletins. If, two weeks ago, you said, "We should have some news in two weeks," then it's time to find out if there is any news. And, if there isn't, say, *"I know I told you we'd have more news by today. But I checked [with the doctors or whatever], and we still don't have anything new."* Then review whatever you do know and let people know what they can do.

Sometimes, it is good to organize some optional group activity related to the situation when the difficulty extends over a long time. One person may visit the patient regularly and report. Or, if the patient can't be seen, the team might make contact with his family or make a donation to a charity in the patient's name. All of these things should be voluntary. Or, some people can share in the cost and everyone can sign the card. This way, no one is pressured, but everyone is included and connected.

Worker's Compensation Claims

Worker's compensation is designed to provide payment to employees injured on the job. But it is more than that—and more complicated. For example, if someone has a chronic condition and it is reinjured or aggravated at work, he may be able to file a claim. Claims can also be made for psychological injury. In addition, when a work-related injury is involved, worker's compensation applies and the Americans with Disabilities Act (ADA) and Family and Medical Leave Act (FMLA) may apply as well.

To put it simply, worker's compensation is too complicated for anyone who is not an HR specialist. This is all the more true because state and city laws vary and because the law is constantly changing. As a manager, *prepare by consulting an expert, keep informed, educate your team, advocate for your team members, and be fair in representing your company.*

Returning to Normal

Crises, by definition, don't last forever. Sooner or later, things return to normal, although—as we've seen with heightened airport security after 9/11—normal may not be what it used to be.

It is best for the company and the team if things return to normal sooner rather than later. If the team has experienced a shock, whether local or national, bring everyone together after a reasonable time. Say, *"Life goes on—but not all by itself. It's our job to make life go on—to do our work, to serve our customers. We can't forget what happened, but it's time to focus on our work."* After a serious tragedy, it is best to do this in stages. For example, it might make sense to meet monthly and, each time, to refocus on work and encourage a return to routine and greater productivity. You can take the same approach when counseling an individual after a personal loss, such as a death in the family.

Chapter 18
Broken Rules

As managers, we stand between the company rules and employee behavior. And the company is governed by rules—laws, regulations, professional standards—as well. In a large company, we are one link in the chain from employee to team, to manager, to HR, to legal department, to the rules of the larger society. We can't keep up with all the rules, but we can—and should—know enough to know when an issue is important enough that we need guidance from the HR or legal departments.

If we work for a smaller company, we don't have that kind of support. Although it is costly, every company should consider retaining an HR consultant and legal counsel as a preventive measure, rather than waiting until a problem arises. As an alternative, there is an excellent book, *The Boss's Survival Guide,* by Bob Rosner, Allan Halcrow, and Alan S. Levins (New York: McGraw-Hill, 2001), that makes an excellent primer for management on these issues.

When we handle difficult situations in our department well, we prevent costly lawsuits and regulatory penalties. To do this, we need to understand the corporate rules and, to some extent, the reasons for them. Some rules are common sense—the business equivalent of "look both ways before you cross the street." Others make sense when you understand the logic, law, or experience behind them—when you know why they are there and what problem they are trying to prevent. And some rules are outmoded—they don't fit the current situation—or they just don't make sense at all.

When we understand the reasons for a rule, it is easier to apply it and to encourage others to abide by it as well. If we agree with the intent of a rule, we can find the most sensible application in a particular situation. For those rules that don't make sense to us, we are ready for difficult situation if we at least understand them and have made our peace with them, so we can decide what to do when they are broken.

One way to prevent difficult situations is to make sure that everyone knows the rules. In fact, training and enforcement on some rules, such as those governing sexual harassment, is key to demonstrating that the business does not tolerate a hostile environment and is therefore not liable for single incidents of abuse. Since miscommunication is a source of conflict, we can prevent difficult situations in general by making sure that everyone is on the same page—of the rule book.

Dress Code Issues

Sometimes, a rule is ignored or forgotten until it becomes a problem. A professional office might assume a dress code and not mention it, until a new employee's revealing outfit, tattoo, or body piercing triggers an unfavorable reaction in a client or around the office.

If someone has complained about someone else's inappropriate or offensive dress or appearance, check the rule book. Ask two questions:

- Does the outfit break the rules?
- Are the rules being followed in general?

If the rules are being followed in general, but this person's appearance is not in accordance with the rules, then meet with the person and say, *"We don't always talk about it, because we all just know it, but we have a dress code. Do you know about it? If not, then I've made a mistake—I should have made sure that you knew."* After you hear the response, describe the specific item—present or past—that doesn't meet the code and ask the person to change it. The person may be able to make a temporary change for the day, such as putting on a sweater to cover an overly revealing top. Unless the clothing is distinctly offensive or dangerous (such as dangling tassels in a machine shop), don't ask the person to go home in the middle of the day to make the change. In general, tomorrow is soon enough.

If the rules are not being followed generally, then your situation is more difficult. Why is what other people doing OK, but this one case is not? Ask that question before the employee does. Then you are ready to say, *"I've looked at the dress code and I've discovered that we all pay less attention to it than we should. But your [item] creates a particular problem for the office."* Talk about the business reason the change is needed and then discuss the change as described in the previous paragraph. You might add, *"It makes sense to create an up-to-date dress code for the department. Would you like to work on it with me?"*

Dress codes go out of date and often include vague terms such as "business casual." If you want to look better at the office or help your team develop a professional appearance, it can make a big difference to the bottom line, even if you aren't in sales. An excellent book on the subject is Dawn E. Waldrop's *Best Impressions: How to Gain Professionalism, Promotion, and Profit* (Cleveland OH: Best Impressions, 1997), available from www.best-impressions.com.

Technology Problems

The ever-changing technology in our offices complicates our lives; some rules can help. In addition to the technical procedures for setting up computers, protecting data from theft and loss, preventing damage due to computer viruses and similar programs, and using software, we also need some general business rules about computers. Here are some suggestions:

- *No sticky foods near computers.* This is one of my favorites, a very practical rule invented by a woman who is far older—and smarter—than any computer. It allows food at the desk while avoiding gumming up the equipment.

- *Only spill-proof cups and mugs near computers.* Have you ever dried out a computer? I have. It isn't pretty.

- *Users should not install their own software* or *Users should not install their own software without guidance and permission.* If you follow the latter rule, have a standard operating procedure for installation and make sure it is updated and verified by a technician for every new operating system.

- *All software must be owned and registered by the company.* This is an issue of legal liability: there have been crackdowns on companies for software piracy.

- *All computers connected to the network must belong to, and be configured and managed by, the company.* This reduces support costs and also reduces the risk of damage due to viruses.

■ *No offensive, pornographic, or adult material or material expressing prejudice or derogatory bias against people or groups of people is allowed on computers or in e-mails.* Make it clear that the company is responsible for all information on its computers and therefore has the right to manage and inspect everything. Employees have no right to privacy of information on office computer systems. This is essential so that the company can demonstrate it is ensuring the absence of a hostile environment in the workplace.

■ *Computers and Internet access are for business use only. Specifically, it is forbidden to use company-owned equipment to browse pornographic or adult sites or other sites containing biased or offensive material.* Be clear that this includes laptops used on the road and at home, if the company owns them.

In particular environments, you may need to add other rules, such as requirements for backing up data and securing systems with passwords. In addition, we can't hold people responsible for the spam e-mails they receive—but we can hold them responsible for the contents of anything they save as well as what they send.

In some offices, it can be a good idea to allow limited, reasonable personal use of computers. For example, if I can phone home to say I'm working late, why can't I do the same by e-mail? If the office allows me to photocopy 10 pages for my child's presentation at school, why can't I print out 10 copies on a computer printer instead? The advantage of allowing reasonable personal use is that it creates a friendlier work environment and builds loyalty. The disadvantage is that it creates a lot of gray areas. How much use is too much? If someone has a flexible lunch hour, how can we be sure that the personal Web browsing that shows up on the log was during lunchtime and not during work hours? If printing for home use is acceptable, what about for church events or political rallies? I am not arguing against a reasonable personal use rule. I'm saying that, whatever rules we make, we have to manage them by informing, educating, and gaining the cooperation of our team.

It is important to take any infraction of these rules seriously and to apply rules consistently and fairly. Otherwise, we run the risk of creating an environment where people's routine habits don't follow the rules. The consequences will be many more difficult situations down the road.

Living with Rules You Don't Like

Sometimes, we have to enforce a rule that we don't agree with. If we've done our best to understand the rule and we can't, we may just have to accept it. The key word is "we." To avoid conflict with your team, say, *"We have to live with this rule."* You might add, *"I probably don't like it much more than you do."* You can also point out that some battles are worth fighting and others aren't. *"Let's live with the rule and focus on the work and our team."*

Unpredictable Rule Changes

In some companies, rules seem to fly out at random from the executives or from HR. It may begin to seem like the company is putting up roadblocks that get in the way of our team, reducing productivity and effectiveness. Even if the rules are good rules, there can still be two problems:

- Each change takes time to learn and implement—and time is money.
- If rules are made without team participation, it is hard to gain understanding and commitment from the team.

One approach is to think of the constantly changing rules as a problem for the team. *"If we want to maintain productivity, we have to deal with these rules changes. Do we want to create a small team within our department to learn the rules when they come in and help us all apply them?"* That way, you delegate some of the work and make compliance more participatory. You might want to have membership on the rules team rotate, so that the workload is balanced and so everyone gets a little taste of management.

Getting Rule Changes

One question that comes up is "Can we—as a team or department—change the rules?" You should discuss this issue with your own boss and with HR. If the company is well organized, it will have clear guidelines for which rules must be applied uniformly, which rules can be interpreted in reasonable ways for different departments, and which rules our teams can choose or create for ourselves.

Unfortunately, the situation is unlikely to be this clear. You may need to advocate for guidance and clarity. When presenting your case, focus on the bottom line—productivity and profit. Rules often reduce risks—such as injury or liability—and that is a good thing. At the same time, different offices have different needs. For example, a travel reimbursement policy that works for most of the company may be a huge burden on a mobile sales force. Here are some ideas to use when you introduce your suggestions:

- Flexibility with clear documentation will keep risks low, while improving productivity.
- The people doing the work know the best ways to do it. Teams that have greater autonomy are not only more productive, but also more compliant with rules that they participate in creating.

If you propose a modified rule, make sure it:

- Enhances productivity
- Serves the functional purpose of the rule it replaces
- Is important enough to take upstairs for approval

Rules Made Up on a Whim

Some rules just don't make any sense at all. So, let's come up with a rule for dealing with those rules: *If no one in the company knows what a rule is for and no one can figure it out, throw out the rule.*

Nonsensical rules waste time and money. Improve performance by getting rid of them.

EXAMPLE: TYING UP A CAT

There is an old story about a teacher who gave lectures in his home. He had a pet cat, which liked to come play with him whenever he gave a talk. Finally, he asked that the cat be tied up during the lectures, so some of the students took care of this.

The old teacher died, but the cat continued to be a nuisance when the new teacher gave a talk, so they continued to tie up the cat.

Then the old cat died. Now, the new teacher didn't want a pet cat. In fact, no one really wanted a cat. But there was this rule—you see—a cat had to be tied up whenever the teacher was going to give a talk. So the students went out and got a cat just so that they could tie it up before every lecture.

The lesson: Unnecessary rules and procedures waste time and money. Don't let them tie you up. Review rules and procedures and keep them current to maximize productivity.

Chapter 19
Respect

When employees respect one another and respect us, it fosters a safe, productive workplace. We can create this environment by modeling it, especially in difficult moments. Respect—which might also be called granting others their dignity—is an attitude, and it must be genuine. We show respect by being present and paying attention fully to each person, by making sure that we understand what he is saying, and by responding thoughtfully, rather than reacting.

Respecting someone doesn't mean always giving him what he wants. But it does mean making sure that he knows he is heard, acknowledged, taken seriously, and appreciated. In fact, when we respect people, it is easier for them to accept that they are not getting exactly what they want.

How do we make respect genuine? By constant practice and by taking good care of ourselves. To express respect clearly, we must not be overwhelmed by tension or difficulty. Then we practice the ingredients listed above, such as attention and awareness. Lastly, we practice specific phrases and methods that communicate respect and make sure that the message gets through.

Respect

Constant respect for others is a very high level of professionalism. It also has other benefits:

- In focusing on respect and appreciation and in working to be responsive, we become less reactive, which reduces our own stress level.
- Often, loyalty and admiration develop as people see how we interact not with them, but with others. When team members see us respecting someone who is angry or shaming, but not giving in to him, their trust in us grows.
- A lack of self-respect is a barrier to respecting others. As we practice respecting others, we give ourselves respect as well, becoming less self-centered and more effective.
- Over time, we build very strong relationships based on mutual respect. This creates room for everyone—ourselves included—to be human and make mistakes without risking the loss of the relationship.

How do we encourage respect as a habit for everyone on our team? It's simple if we take these three steps:

1. First, we model respect all the time.
2. We ask for respect—not particularly for ourselves—rather, we ask the team to respect one another, ourselves, customers, everyone.
3. We teach how to respect, using tools in this chapter and other tools we have found to be effective.

How do we know when our respect for others is working? People simply tell us. They let us know how much we are appreciated and how much they feel supported by us.

A team with mutual respect lasts a long time, with low cost, high productivity, and an opportunity for everyone to make a creative contribution to common goals.

Communication

When people want something, they actually want two things, because all communication is two-way. First, we want to be heard. Second, we want whatever we want. Now, as a listener and a boss, I can't always give you what you want. But I can always make sure that you are heard and that you know it.

Whenever you refuse a request, say, *"I understand how you feel, but ...."* If a person is upset, then slow it down even further. Say, *"I understand you feel ...."* Then stop, listen, and make sure that he knows he is heard and that he is relaxing. After that, tell him the bad news that he is not getting what he wants.

If the situation is confusing and the person is confused as well as upset, we can slow things down even further by using a technique called *mirroring*. To use mirroring, follow these steps:

1. Listen.
2. Say, *"What I hear you say is ..."* and then repeat back his ideas in your own words. Then ask, *"Did I get that right?"*
3. Have him correct anything you said or tell you that you got it right.
4. Give your response.

You can ask people on your team to mirror you, as well. That way, you can be sure that they understand you or that they are clear on complicated directions. If people are very upset, it helps if everyone uses mirroring and if each person speaks very briefly—just a sentence or two—before the mirroring.

It may seem like an awful lot of effort, but it really isn't. We all do it all the time, when we're asking for directions to a place we don't know. Why? Because we want to get it right and we don't want to spend time getting lost and finding our way. Mirroring eliminates so much frustration and saves so much time that would be lost to misunderstandings that it pays for itself—with benefits.

The "Yes and ..." Response

"Yes, and ..." is the simplest trick I know for expressing respect and preventing arguments. Read both of these dialogs aloud and see if you can hear the difference:

"I deserve a raise."

"I know you think you deserve a raise, but no, you're not going to get one."

That could become an argument. Now, try this one:

"I deserve a raise."

"Yes, I understand you feel you deserve a raise. And I'm sorry, but you're not going to get one right now."

I've added a few other things that express, on the written page, the feeling of *"Yes, and ...."* "Understand" is gentler than "know." "Yes" is gentler than "no." Acknowledging feelings, apologizing, and setting a time limit so that it doesn't seem like you're being absolute all build relationship and reduce tension.

When we make a habit of saying, *"Yes, and ...,"* these other gentle expressions come naturally and we foster a relationship based on respect, reducing tension. As a team, we learn how to have disagreement without disagreeable conflict.

Respect, Please

Some behaviors—such as interrupting people who are speaking, changing the topic, rolling your eyes in disbelief, or walking out of the room while someone is talking to you—are gestures that signify disrespect, whether intended or not. If you see people doing these things or if a team member complains that he is not being respected, identify the behavior and talk to the person who did it. Be sure that the person really does this, and it happens often, before you confront him.

"I hope you respect everyone on the team and I'm asking you to act as if you do. When you [say or do whatever], people think you are not being respectful." Then ask if the person is aware of the behavior and if he is willing to try to change it. Here is how to deal with some common responses:

- "But so-and-so said ...." Reply, *"Even so, maturity is how we act around immature people. Please be professional and respectful. If you like, I'll ask the other person to do the same."*
- "I didn't know I did that." Reply, *"Sometimes, it's hard to catch ourselves doing these things. If I see it again, would you like me to take you aside and let you know?"*

We can discuss respect with the whole team, but we should never ask one person to change a behavior or to be more respectful in front of others. That sounds like you are calling the person immature and it can be very shaming. When we have been shamed, it is much harder to see and change our own behavior.

Making Room for Differences

Part of respect is to allow room for people to have views, thoughts, and feelings—and, of course, physical appearance and preferences—different from our own. Yet many of us argue, criticize, or nag as if we want others to agree with us or be just like us. There is much to be said this statement, attributed incorrectly to Voltaire: *"I disapprove of what you say, but I will defend to the death your right to say it."*

Encourage your team: *"Let everyone speak freely, without being criticized. Express respect and appreciation before you disagree."* You can follow up by teaching tools such as team brainstorming to create ground rules from Chapter 5, When Sex Shows Up at Work, and brainstorming without put-downs from Chapter 7, Pranks, Put-Downs, and Bending the Rules.

When a Team Member Doesn't Listen

What do you do when a team member complains about another team member, "He just doesn't listen"? First, ask the person making the complaint for specific examples. Make sure the person is being clear and try to work out what is really going on. When we say someone isn't listening, we might mean that the person is:

- not remembering things and not writing them down to make sure they get done
- not doing what we want him to do
- inattentive, actually not listening
- allowing interruptions and distractions, such as answering the phone during a meeting

Once you have worked out what is actually going on, decide on what needs to be changed. Here are some possibilities:

- Work requests and instructions should always be written down.
- People should be encouraged to speak freely about their unwillingness to do a particular job.
- People should be required to tell someone in a timely fashion if they cannot do a requested task.
- The person needs training in listening skills.
- The team needs ground rules for not allowing interruptions during meetings.

Decide which action is appropriate and guide the person or the team to an effective solution.

Men, Women, Culture, and Respect

When men and women talk to one another, signals can get crossed and people can feel disrespected even when no disrespect is intended. The same is true across cultures. We don't see or hear our own choices of words, facial expressions, patterns of listening and speaking, and body language. That makes it hard to change them. Yet these expressions mean different things to different people.

Here are two examples:

- Each of us pauses a certain amount of time between thoughts or sentences. People who use shorter pauses assume others do as well. As a result, they think that others are finished speaking when the other person is still thinking—and they interrupt. In general, men speak with shorter pauses, so men tend to interrupt women by mistake more often.

- In some American culture today, women are very offended by whistles, catcalls, and other male expressions appreciating their beauty or sexual attractiveness. In fact, such actions can be the basis for a sexual harassment claim. At the same time, there are cultures where these same expressions are not only done by men, but also appreciated by women. In some cultures, women take pride in their appearance and like having it acknowledged.

These patterns are studied in the field of sociolinguistics. A good practical book about men, women, and communication at work is Deborah Tannen's *You Just Don't*

Understand: Women and Men in Conversation (New York: Perennial Currents, 2001).

When a person feels disrespected, make sure to ask, *"Exactly what is the other person doing that makes you feel that way?"* Then work the situation out with the two people. It may be useful to build new ground rules or it may be best just to help the person accept the other person's behavior and understand that no disrespect is intended.

EXAMPLE: TRANSLATING ACROSS CULTURES

My grandparents grew up in New York City. One time—this was back in the 1940s—they were visiting a woman their own age from rural North Carolina. My grandmother and the other woman literally could not understand what the other person was saying. Their English was perfectly good, but their accents were too different. My grandfather, who could understand both of them, repeated what each of them said slowly, so that they could understand one another.

Now, my grandfather and grandmother grew up together and had the same accent. How was it that he could understand a Southern accent when his wife couldn't? He was a college professor. He had learned to speak slowly in order to be understood and to listen carefully to people with different accents.

The lesson: Whether it is a matter of accents, gestures, words, tone of voice, or body language, we should learn to listen to each person and understand him or her. We should work to make ourselves understood patiently, without criticism as well. And we can guide our team to do the same.

Part Three

Too Hot to Handle

What is better than perfect solutions to difficult situations? That's easy—preventing difficult situations altogether. Well, it's easy to say, but it's not easy to do. However, if we can prevent difficult situations, it is more cost-effective than running around putting out fires. Instead of solving difficult situations, we can spend our time looking ahead and making improvements.

Some difficult situations will always come up. But there is a lot we can do to prevent them and a lot we can do to make sure we can handle them well when they happen.

In Chapter 20, When to Get Help, we look at the support we can get from two types of expertise: human resources departments (or consulting services) and legal guidance. In a large company, we can turn to an HR department or legal counsel. In smaller companies, we might need to look for outside consultants. Either way, it helps to know two things: What can we do proactively to prevent issues from needing HR or legal support? And, how do we know when a situation is getting beyond what a manager should try to take care alone?

In Chapter 21, Learning Leadership, we turn to the qualities of leadership that we can learn and practice so that we can train each team member to be more independent and resourceful. That way, when there's a difficult situation, the employee will come to you and say, "I already took care of it."

Chapter 20
When to Get Help

S ome office problems require authority or expertise beyond what you, as a manager or supervisor, can or should handle. The challenge is to know when those moments have arrived. You don't want things to get out of hand. You also don't want to pass the buck on jobs that really are your responsibility.

What Managers Do

Let's think of a company as being squished between legal problems at one end and employee problems at the other. The problems fall into three categories.

- *Criminal charges* that arise from a company violating laws, either intentionally, or through neglect of its legal responsibilities

- *General civil charges* arising from general corporate practices that violate employees' individual rights or violate regulatory standards

- *Individual civil charges,* where an individual employee charges the company with a violation of his civil rights

Large companies manage the problem of being squished by legal and employee problems with a set of three shock absorbers, each with a different function. The first shock absorber is the legal department, which responds to criminal and civil charges, and advises regarding the risk or vulnerability to those charges. The human resources department acts as the second shock absorber by defining and implementing policies about staff that reduce the risk of legal trouble.

We managers are the third shock absorber. Our work has three major effects: improving productivity, retaining staff, and reducing the risk of legal and regulatory problems. Here are some things we can do as managers to reduce those risks:

- Gain a general awareness of employee and company rights, the laws that cover them, and the most common problem areas.
- Get specific training in any area that is important to our business, including general topics, such as sexual harassment and employee health care, and industry-specific topics.
- Build a team with a no-blame environment and a lot of respect. One major motivation for lawsuits—as opposed to less expensive conflict resolution methods—is a perception that the manager or the company disrespects employees or is unwilling to take responsibility or to accept blame.
- Learn from human resources and legal resources proactively about how to prevent problems, instead of waiting for a problem to happen.
- Watch for signs of abnormal or extreme conflict and consult with HR or legal resources early in managing these conflicts.

■ Be aware of the limitations of your own knowledge and ask for guidance before you act on anything that confuses you or that may have implications for employee rights or company liability.

If your company has a legal department or legal counsel and has a human resources department, then that's where to go for help. But what if you work for or own a small company without those resources? Then you need to turn to consulting services for help. Here are some tips.

■ Even a one-person company should have someone to discuss legal concerns such as incorporation and contracts. If that company gets employees, use that lawyer for employee-related advice as well. Make sure the lawyer has a practice working with small firms and understands their cost limitations and issues. If possible, find someone with knowledge of your industry.

■ As soon as a company has even one employee, it should take care to set up a good payroll system. Payroll errors are very costly and corporate owners or officers are held personally liable for violations, which can lead to personal financial liability or even time in jail. This can be done through a CPA or a firm specializing in payroll services. However, it's a good idea to get someone with experience and training in HR with a specialty in small businesses.

■ As a company grows to a few employees, more knowledge of HR is extremely valuable. Some basic HR knowledge can help avoid bad hiring choices, improve retention, and keep you out of legal hot water.

■ State and local laws vary greatly and the laws change frequently. Reading this book—or any book—is not a good substitute for legal and HR expertise. To get things right, you need to be able to review your particular situation with someone who knows the applicable legal responsibilities, rights, laws, regulations, and precedents.

Danger Signs

Obviously, we do not want to run for help every time a team member has a problem. At the same time, news stories about the rare cases when an employee goes berserk without warning have us worried that we will not escalate a problem when we should. As a first step, check with your HR and legal departments and see if they have guidelines for when they want to be informed. In addition, consider these guidelines:

In general, *do not* escalate an issue under the following conditions:

- It is clear what the problem is, and
- You and the team member(s) involved have a plan for a solution, and
- Everyone is cooperating toward the solution, and
- It appears it can be worked out without anyone leaving the company.

Here are some reasons to notify HR and get them involved:

- There is a possibility that the situation will lead to termination and you want to follow proper procedure and document it properly. Termination of an employee, even when done for good reason, can be overturned by a legal challenge if it is not done properly, with objective reasons, warnings of possible termination, and adequate time to correct the problem properly documented.

- An employee has or might have a medical issue. Becoming aware of a medical diagnosis—by figuring it out, by hearing about it from the employee, or by hearing about it from someone else—changes a company's obligations under the Americans with Disabilities Act (ADA).

- An employee has or might have a substance abuse problem with alcohol or drugs or a behavioral addiction, such as gambling. These conditions create several risks to the office environment. First of all, addiction is very hard to cure, so a good resolution is less likely. Second, addicts often become very good at hiding the truth, so honesty and trust—essential ingredients to any good solution—are compromised. Third, drug testing is a legal quagmire. Last, people with drug or alcohol problems who are in treatment or recovering afterwards may be entitled to special treatment under the ADA.

- You simply feel that you're in over your head or that something odd is going on and you can't figure out what. I've learned that experience and expertise matter. Your expertise is in managing your department. Don't hesitate to consult with and learn from someone with a different expertise—human resource issues.

Here are some reasons to get the HR or legal department involved and let them guide the process:

- You know that relevant rules exist and you know you don't know enough about them. Sometimes, we know we don't know the basics, such as how unemployment compensation works. Other times, we run across a situation where we've never dealt with the legal issues before. Perhaps it is the first time a team member has been injured on the job; we know what worker's compensation is, but we've never had to deal with it.

- There is the possibility of a legal claim, whether administrative, civil, or criminal.
- You yourself are part of the conflict and your own efforts to resolve it aren't going well. Mediation by a third party can help.

In making the decision to ask for help, use common sense, but it is better to err on the side of asking—of more communication—rather than keeping silent. If you're worried that, in your work environment, asking for guidance may make you look weak, then here's what you can do. First, define the problem clearly. Second, propose a direction or a solution. Third, approach HR or the legal department as one expert to another, saying, *"I've outlined this plan of action, but I want to check it with you first. I know that there may be procedures or legal rules that I'm not aware of."* That way, you are establishing a basis that says, "We are both professionals here, but we have different areas of expertise." In my own experience, I've found that most HR people and legal counselors are there to help by providing their perspective and expertise, not to criticize.

Another approach to the same problem is *"This situation is becoming difficult and I wanted to make sure you were in the loop."* Here, you are doing the responsible thing and informing HR or legal counsel. The worst they can say is "This problem is too small for us." Then you can ask what criteria to apply in the future. In any case, the chances you will be criticized or blamed for raising the issue are much less.

I encourage more communication, rather than less, for a simple reason. The consequences of problems where HR or legal counsel didn't know until too late are much worse than the consequences of them knowing about a trivial problem too soon. If we go back to the analogy I used at the beginning of this chapter, a company needs all three shock absorbers to keep from getting squished by a big crunch. If you don't bring in HR or legal counsel before you hit the big bump, the company is running on one shock absorber—just you—and the damage will be worse. In fact, the damage will probably be worse especially for you.

Establish good relationships with HR and legal counsel, learn from them, and keep them informed as particularly difficult situations evolve.

The lesson: HR often has solutions in place for problems we don't know how to fix. And the legal department can often take us through routine procedures to handle difficult situations. That's what they're paid to do; that's what they're there for.

Avoiding Lawsuit and Scandal

Every person in this country has the right to initiate a lawsuit on any grounds that he or she thinks are reasonable. As a result, there is nothing a company can do to ensure that lawsuits won't be filed. However, there are many things we can do to reduce the chances of a lawsuit. Lawyers call this *reducing our exposure* to a legal action.

- Maintain good relationships with employees. Be respectful and resolve conflicts promptly and fairly. People get angry—and are more likely to take action—when they feel they are not being listened to. There is even some evidence that companies that apologize are less likely to be sued.
- Follow procedures, be consistent, and keep written records

created at the time you take action. Most HR procedures are designed to ensure compliance with laws and regulations. If things do get to court, consistency, fairness, and a clear, documented record of timely effort to resolve problems go a long way to helping your case.

■ Ensure good communication, even during a conflict. Listen well, ask people what they need from you, give it to them, and get acknowledgment—preferably written—that they've gotten what they need. Have written evidence that they were given a clear chance and knew the consequences. That's where the phrase "disciplinary action, up to and including termination" comes in.

■ Make use of additional resources. Mediation and arbitration are much less expensive than legal action and administrative courts are less expensive than the regular judicial system.

In some cases, a company may be concerned about public-

The Protection of Arbitration

Arbitration is the process of having a formal arbitrator, rather than a judge, resolve disputes. It saves a great deal of cost. However, given that everyone has the right to sue in court, we can't push a person into arbitration after a problem arises. Therefore, it is a good idea to include an arbitration clause in all contracts and appropriate employee agreements. To learn more about arbitration or get the language for an arbitration clause, contact the American Arbitration Association at www.adr.org.

ADR is *alternative dispute resolution* and it includes *arbitration*, where the parties work with an arbitrator who has authority to make a binding decision, and *mediation*, where

> the parties work with a mediator, but the mediator does not have the authority to make the decision binding.

ity regarding an unresolved issue. Bad publicity is a costly problem; it includes:

- Rumors—or accurate reports—of actions that reflect badly on the company circulating within the company
- Similar news circulating among customers
- Unfavorable reports in newspapers, magazines, television, or other media

Bad publicity—deserved or not—damages a company's reputation. The best ways to prevent it are through respectful communication and prompt ownership of responsibility for our side of an issue. The lesson: Be respectful, take the no-blame approach, and own your mistakes promptly to develop and maintain a solid reputation.

Maybe This Employee Needs Professional Help

"Professional help" is a common euphemism for psychological or psychiatric care. We all have days when we think other people need it—and probably some days where we could use a little help ourselves. But we are not qualified to decide whether an employee needs psychological support or even assistance with a substance abuse problem or addiction.

If you work for a large company, find out if your company offers an employee assistance program (EAP), which is a structured program of psychological, substance abuse, addiction, and other support services for employees. If your company has one, the program administrators will offer guidelines in how to recommend that an employee reach out to them for help or go for counseling.

It is important to separate substance abuse problems from psychological disorders, even though the two often go together. Employers should have clear policies with relation to substance abuse at work, criminal activities (such as possession of illegal drugs) at work, and working while under the influence of substances. Some companies, such as construction, where public safety is involved, must have these rules in place.

Here are some things to keep in mind in relation to substance abuse:

- Having a clear policy—and being familiar with it—are a big help.
- Many companies will help an employee who comes for assistance voluntarily, but fire an employee who is caught using or under the influence of alcohol or drugs.
- Knowing if a problem exists (knowing, as opposed to suspecting), without violating an employee's right to privacy, is very difficult.
- Searching employees or their purses, clothing, or lockers can be a violation of privacy. Companies should have a written rule, reviewed by legal counsel, in place—and signed by the employee on hiring—that the company has a right to search desks, all office areas, computer systems, and all written documentation. Since companies are responsible for ensuring that a workplace is not a hostile environment, we need to establish clear authority to look for signs of a hostile environment in the workplace. Such a policy is also helpful in relation to finding evidence of substance abuse.
- Companies should have a policy in place that discovery of

an employee committing a crime during work hours or on company property is grounds for immediate termination, as this covers substance abuse during work hours, driving under the influence during work hours, and holding or selling illegal drugs on company property.

■ Testing employees for substance abuse raises very complicated legal issues. (See the sidebar below.)

When a team member is unable to resolve a difficult situation

Drug Testing Troubles

A drug test is an invasion of personal privacy and can be a violation of our constitutional right not to be subject to illegal search and seizure. A person can take drugs on his personal time. This is a crime and something of a concern to an employer, but it is fundamentally none of our business. When we test for drugs, even during working hours, we can detect drugs taken on personal time—and we're not allowed to know about that.

Also, suspicion of drug use is not adequate grounds for testing, because people may have biased reasons for suspecting one person and not suspecting someone else.

Since drug addiction generally includes a tendency to hide the activity or even lie about it—especially to those who can take away your job or get you arrested—companies and managers often find themselves in the awkward situation of not being able to find out something we really need to know: does an employee have a substance abuse problem or addiction?

Companies in transportation and construction have

highly structured, regulated programs for managing these issues. One solution—a bit expensive and possibly not a good match for your corporate culture—is to have the same policy in place in your own company. An HR consultant can help a company develop and implement these policies.

Sometimes, though, a small company has never thought to be concerned about these issues or hasn't felt that such a program is affordable. One small business ran into trouble with an employee suspected of a drug problem. Their ultimate solution was first to implement a policy that a person could be terminated for use of illegal drugs and then to test everyone in the company. It was expensive, but it established the fairness necessary to hold up in court. Even this solution may not be applicable in all situations, so if you find yourself in the situation where the problem arrives before the policy, be sure to consult professionals who are experts in the human resources and legal issues related to substance abuse.

even when given a defined goal, clear steps, and supportive coaching, then clearly there is either a lack of motivation or some barrier to success. If the problem is a lack of motivation, then our job as managers is to clarify the situation to the point where the employee knows the consequences of his actions and either gets motivated or not. We respond to whatever the employee does. If the employee gets motivated, the difficult situation is resolved. If the employee does not get motivated, then we have three choices: we live with the problem, we change the situation (for example, by reassigning the team member), or we let the employee go.

If the problem is a barrier to success, then that barrier is in communications, in management, or psychological. The solutions throughout this book address communications and management barriers and help you to remove them. If a problem remains after you've done your best, it may well be psychological. What do we mean when we say an employee has a psychological problem? We mean that, due to some inner mental or emotional issue, the employee is unable to perform work in a situation where a reasonable and capable employee could perform the work.

A situation that seems simple to us but doesn't resolve after

What If It's Me?

Sometimes a team member can't resolve a situation because his boss—that's you or me—has a psychological problem. What do we do if our own quirks—a habit of getting angry or a tendency to avoid facing issues clearly—prevent our team members from doing their job?

First of all, it helps to approach ourselves without judgment or blame. We all have our issues and difficulties. Every character type has strengths and flaws. In plain English, direct people tend to get angry and gentle people tend to be indirect. And both anger and indirectness cause problems for our team.

If a team member accuses us of having a psychological problem or if we become concerned, a good first step is to talk with either trusted friends or a counselor. A fresh perspective is very supportive. When I've done this, I've found that one of three things happens—and all of them are good:

- *Affirmation.* The colleague or counselor offers perspec-

> tive, saying that we actually are right on track, we are being reasonable, and we can return to the situation with new confidence.
>
> ■ *A different perspective.* Sometimes, a fresh ear offers a fresh voice. The person may see things in a really different way that helps reduce the tension or makes a solution clear.
>
> ■ *Support.* If, indeed, we are overstressed or need to look at a deeper issue, then it is good that we stepped forward and asked someone we trusted. Then we need to muster the courage for the next step—facing the problem and getting the help we need.

several tries, even though the employee is committed and willing and is a good match for the job, is a sign of possible psychological symptoms. What are some others?

- Any sign of severe stress, such as unexplained absence from work or prolonged inability to focus
- Inability to understand simple directions
- Inability to do productive work
- Stress in ourselves. Oddly enough, due to empathy—the ability to feel what others are feeling—one sign of a team member's psychological imbalance is our reaction to him or her. If I find myself getting upset or confused every time I'm with someone—or just after I see him—and I can find no reason in myself, it may be a sign that the person is having a problem.

A psychological disorder is not grounds for disciplinary

Understanding Psychological Symptoms

These days, people use way too much psychological language. We say, "I'm depressed," when we really mean, "I feel sad." As managers, we need to understand two things.

First, psychological symptoms are simply more severe or longer-lasting versions of feelings we all have. We all have moods and changes of moods. Psychological problems involve very strong moods, severe mood swings, or the inability to get out of a particular mood. We all think about things and do things. When someone can't stop thinking and doing certain things, that's a psychological problem called obsessive-compulsive disorder (OCD, like *Monk* on TV). And so forth.

Second, psychological symptoms may arise from a number of causes; psychological disorders are just one possible cause. Here are some common sources of psychological or mental symptoms, with examples:

- *Healthy psychological processes.* If a person loses a parent, a spouse, a family member, or even a pet, that is grieving, which is a healthy process, even though the symptoms are similar to depression.
- *Physical brain disorders.* Attention deficit disorder (ADD) and attention deficit hyperactivity disorder (ADHD) exist in adults as well as children and are a significant source of work-related problems. People with these conditions do not have a psychological problem; they have a brain chemical disorder.
- *Side effects of medication.* A team member may be on

223

medication that induces drowsiness, an inability to focus, anxiety, or other mental symptoms.

- *Allergies.* Allergies—to pollen, chemicals, or food—can have symptoms such as rage attacks, hyperactivity, and an inability to focus.

- *Illnesses and pain.* Illnesses such as hypoglycemia—low blood sugar—can cause an inability to focus. Physical pain, caused by illness or injury, can lead to an inability to focus on work.

- *Chronic stress* can lead to psychological symptoms. The true solution is to alleviate the stress, whether it is at work or at home. The stressful situation may itself be psychological—as some marital problems are—or may be physical or social, as when an employee is taking care of a critically ill family member.

- *Mental injury.* The most severe form of mental injury is post-traumatic stress disorder (PTSD), which we normally associate with experiencing physical abuse, surviving an attack, or witnessing the horror of war or terrorism. But PTSD can also arise as a result of mental injury in the workplace, including mobbing and discrimination. As managers, we should work to create a healthy, no-blame work environment where these problems do not arise. We should also watch out for evidence that employees may be enduring or have survived abuse that affects their ability to perform at work.

- *Psychological illness.* If psychological symptoms exist and are not due to any of the other causes listed, then the person may have a psychological illness such as depression, obsessive-compulsive disorder, or bipolar disorder (formerly called manic depression). Such issues can be treated and managed through therapy and medication.

The lesson: The field of psychological symptoms and their causes is extremely important. We can't help our team members much in this area ourselves, because we don't know enough and because helping them requires knowing personal things that we, as their bosses, should not know. If a problem escalates beyond what the office can handle, then we should encourage the employees to get whatever assistance might help—and keep that recommendation vague, rather than specific. If you have any stories about how seeing a doctor or counselor helped you or someone you know, share them, for two reasons: to avoid getting involved in the employee's own situation and to encourage the idea that getting help we need is normal and healthy.

action or termination. In fact, if we become aware of an employee's diagnosis, we may be required to accommodate that disability under the Americans with Disabilities Act. This creates an awkward situation. An employee may be pressured to keep a diagnosis private, for fear of reprisal, harassment, or criticism, and yet may also feel pressured to come out and tell the employer, in order to receive the protection of the ADA. For this reason, HR should be involved when psychological illness—or any chronic illness—seems to be at issue.

However, HR is only part of the solution. Here are some things we managers can do with regard to an employee's psychological issues:

- Maintain clear, objective job descriptions that require specific behavior and clearly defined attitudes. This can help establish business reasons for requiring change—or terminating an employee, if necessary—independently of psychological or substance abuse diagnoses.
- Reduce stress in the office by giving people clearly defined work and appropriate rewards.
- Take an active role in encouraging compliance with sexual harassment, diversity, anger management, stress reduction, and other relevant training programs.
- Maintain good, regular contact with your team at least weekly. Have an open door policy. Resolve difficult situations on your team—whether personal or interpersonal—promptly and fairly.
- Care but don't infantilize. Treat your team members as adults. Simply be a caring person who also respects each person's ability to care for himself or herself and resolve problems.

Compassionate Management

Life is a flow of joy—and full of problems. As managers, our primary focus should be on productivity, on work and results. At the same time, people will come to us with problems, especially if we keep an open door and express respect for people and confidence in their ability to solve problems.

In relation to difficult situations in general, our focus should be on prevention and on catching problems early. When situations arise—and, as long as companies have employees, they will—we should approach them without blame, with respect for the team member who will need to solve the problem—and who has the capacity to do so.

Also, balance is important. We need to be able to raise issues and support team members in their efforts to find solutions without making their problems our own. We have enough of our own problems and, when we are done with our problems, we have plenty of good work to do. In the best of work environments, everyone grows together, solving our own problems and moving on to take on new challenges.

Chapter 21
Learning Leadership

What is the point of coming up with perfect solutions? Is it just so that we can get through our day a little better and remove a few roadblocks for our team? No, it is more than that. Offering a perfect solution to a difficult situation builds up our team's confidence in us. And it frees our time to move from managing—preventing and solving problems—to leading.

A leader is someone who has followers. Will your team follow you? Will they make an extra effort when thing get tough? Will the more experienced employees try new things and the younger ones be willing to do it your way? Will each person on the team become self-managed, contribute creative ideas, and then work together under your guidance to move in new directions? To the extent that these things are happening, you are a leader.

A good office is a successful team. A successful team has two basic qualities: the ability to achieve goals and the ability to work together. As the leader of our team, we set direction—defining the goals—and we create and nourish teams.

In this chapter, we explore five essential leadership skills:

- *Setting direction.* With input from the team, we define a set of goals that are good for the company and our customers. Then we inspire the team to meet those goals—and improve on them.
- *Communicating and acting.* Communication comes up with good ideas—good solutions to problems. But we also need to know how to move from knowing the good solution to implementing it, moving into action and ensuring that the good idea becomes a reality.
- *Helping people motivate themselves.* If we try to motivate our team, we will fail—and we will burn out. But we can help our team focus on the job and connect with their own desire to do good work
- *Creating and nourishing a team.* A team is a living thing. We need to bring the right people together, give them what they need, trim their rough edges and train their habits, and replace or add people so the team can stay strong and grow.
- *Expanding horizons.* When a team is working really well, with good leadership, it will grow and it can be a source for innovations and improvements.

Setting Direction

In any company, the executive function sets strategy. *Strategy* begins with values—what matters to the company—and defines the goals that add value. If you help set goals for your company or your team, you are part of the strategic process. And if you include your team members, you are including them in the strategy, as well. Companies that let managers and teams provide input into strategies tend to succeed. Their goals are more realistic, because the team members who know what the work is really like have had a hand in the process. Also, the teams are more highly motivated, because they have a hand in setting the direction.

If your company doesn't give you a chance to set strategy, you still have a job to do: *set the direction for your team*. Setting the direction for your team includes:

- Defining goals in simple language and making sure everyone understands those goals
- Prioritizing and scheduling those goals, so that people know what to do when, and so that deadlines and quotas are met
- Helping team members understand and be motivated to do their part to achieve goals and quotas
- Taking a proactive and responsive stance—a can-do attitude—by removing roadblocks so your team can meet its goals.

All of these activities are good leadership. They also model good leadership, showing your team how to become more effective—by example.

Communicating and Acting

When I teach management classes, I have a very hard time convincing people that effective meetings are possible—but they are. Usually, in a class of 30 people, just one person will have experienced effective meetings and seen the difference they make. But, for anyone who has seen the difference, we know that effective meetings make all the difference. When we have effective meetings with our team, we catch and resolve situations before they even become difficult.

We can ensure effective meetings by taking three steps:

- *Define clear goals for every meeting* by delivering an agenda in advance.
- *Have effective communications feedback.* Using techniques such as mirroring and active listening, ensure that each person understands the person who is speaking.
- *Have effective feedback to control future actions.* A meeting doesn't end with good ideas—or the good ideas will end in the meeting. Each idea needs to become a decision and then an action item.

An action item has these elements: a person who takes responsibility for doing the job, a description of the job, a goal, and a delivery date. A meeting that ends with action items has an effect—is effective—because it changes the work we are going to do, so that we solve difficult situations and get better results.

The Two Levels of Feedback

Not too long ago, I ordered dinner at a Chinese restaurant. The waiter was excellent at active listening and effective level-one feedback for communications. I asked for appetizer #6, and he said, "The chicken with lettuce?" and I told him he had that right. Then I ordered our main dishes.

The main dishes came, but there was no appetizer. After a few minutes, I hailed the waiter and asked what had happened. He checked his charge slip and apologized profusely. He had forgotten to put the order in for the appetizer. He missed level-two feedback—actions that deliver the desired result.

The lesson: Good understanding isn't enough—we also have to take action and deliver the desired results.

Helping People Motivate Themselves

Here are seven things we can do to help people motivate themselves:

- Define jobs clearly, with a starting point, an ending point, and clear directions.
- Let team members know the consequences of success and failure for the company.
- Provide incentives. Make sure that the consequences for team members are aligned with corporate goals and let team members know the consequences of success and failure for themselves.
- Remove roadblocks. If something not under the employee's control gets in the way, get it out of the way.
- Praise small successes.
- Let people plan their own work and decide for themselves the best way to do a job.
- Increase autonomy. As team members succeed, give them larger jobs, more complicated jobs, and more say in what they do and how they do it.

Creating and Nourishing a Team

As our team members become more independent and communicate better, the team grows stronger. There is an important quality called *robustness*. A team is robust when it can handle unexpected changes of direction and setbacks, adjust well, and stay on course—or set a new course, if necessary. If individual team members are set in their ways and uncooperative, a team can't become robust. On the other hand, if each team member enjoys a challenge, likes to face new situations, and is willing to do his share of the boring work to get the job done, then a team will be robust.

Assess your team:

- *Does the team, as a whole, have the skills and knowledge to do the job?* If not, add to the team's abilities through training or through adding another person.
- *Is the team flexible?* Do team members know one another's jobs well enough to substitute for each other when someone is absent? Are they willing to do it? Or do they insist on only doing their own jobs?
- *Is the team strong?* Can the team handle an occasional extra workload? Or is everyone already pushed to the max? If a company runs its teams in continuous overload, it will run into trouble in the long run.

In creating a team, pick people who have the technical skills to do the job and who also have the ability to get along with one another. In developing a team, continue to focus on those qualities. Key qualities are:

- The ability to listen
- The ability to express ideas, in writing, one on one, or to groups
- Self-management: the ability to take on a job and deliver good results on time with available resources

The solutions throughout this book model, teach, and encourage self-management. In our culture, listening is a skill that is inadequately trained and cultivated. As a result, teaching everyone to listen well has huge benefits for a team. Once people listen well, they become a good audience. That makes it easier to help people express ideas better. In general, each person has a preferred mode of communication—writing, speaking to one person, or speaking to groups—and it is best to have a team member use that strength first. If a person is committed to professional development, then learning a new skill of expression—outward communication, such as becoming a better writer or public speaker—is a rewarding challenge.

Expanding Horizons

When we are robust and ready to handle whatever comes at us, we are ready to grow—and the same is true of our teams. When communication is easy and fluid and team members do their jobs and help one another, then the team can do more. What more? Well, what does the company need? Does it make sense to focus on product improvements, to increase productivity, to solve some longstanding project, or to launch a new venture?

I don't know—but I bet your team does. When a team is working this well, it becomes a source for innovations and improvements. You can grow with your team by leading brainstorming sessions focused on strategy—that is, on setting new directions for the work and the team.

Individuals will grow, as well. You and members of your team may receive promotions to new jobs or new departments. You will be working with new people, doing new things. And, inevitably, you will run into problems and be looking for the perfect solution to a difficult situation.

Chapter 22
Resources for Learning

Perfect Solutions for Difficult Employee Situations is just a beginning for those of you who want to become better managers and leaders. My company, Quality Technology & Instruction, maintains two Web sites with more resources—articles, tools, and forms—that support effective management. You can find supplements, updates, and additions to this book at **www.qualitytechnology.com/books/psdes.htm**. You can find more materials for managers and workers at *www.LivingJoy.net/JobJoy.htm*, which offers a set of emotional intelligence tools based on the idea that life is a flow of joy, full of problems.

Sid tours nationally, offering speeches, lectures, book signings, and consulting services. He also offers executive coaching in person and over the phone. For more information, come to our Web site at *www.qualitytechnology.com*. Sid also loves to hear suggestions and corrections for his books, and talk with his readers about anything, so don't hesitate to be in touch by e-mail at sid@qualitytechnology.com.

Sid has written two other books that might be of interest: *Project Management Demystified* (McGraw-Hill, 2004), which offers best practices for leading a team to deliver high quality results on time and under budget, and *Budgeting for Managers* (McGraw-Hill 2002), which introduces managers to the basics of planning and keeping income and expense budgets.

The following books were mentioned in this text:

Mobbing: Emotional Abuse in the American Workplace, by Noa Davenport, Ruth Distler Schwartz, and Gail Purcell Elliot (Civil Society Publishing, 1999), available at *www.mobbing-usa.com,* is the most definitive book on mobbing, or bullying, in the American workplace.

Somebodies and Nobodies: Overcoming the Abuse of Rank, by Robert W. Fuller (New Society Publishers, 2003), is a book that explores the problems created when people misuse the power granted by rank, title, or position.

The Boss's Survival Guide, by Bob Rosner, Allan Halcrow, and Alan S. Levins (McGraw-Hill, 2001), is a particularly good primer regarding the laws and regulations that managers should be aware of.

You Just Don't Understand: Women and Men in Conversation by Deborah Tannen (Perennial Currents, 2001), is a valuable and enjoyable exploration of how men and women inevitably misinterpret one another because we use language differently. It is very valuable for anyone wanting to improve ability for working with—or managing—men and women together.

Best Impressions: How to Gain Professionalism, Promotion, and Profit, by Dawn E. Waldrop, is available from *www.best-impressions.com.* This little book demystifies vague terms such as "business casual" and teaches anyone how to use clothing and accessories to succeed in a business environment.